Dementia Dolls

Dementia Dolls
A Daughter's Story

Mary Ann Kampfe

E. L. Marker
Salt Lake City

Published by E.L. Marker, an imprint of WiDo Publishing

WiDō Publishing
Salt Lake City, Utah
widopublishing.com

Author photo by Carol Bruno
Cover photo by Salvatore Mina
Cover design by Steven Novak
Book design by Marny K. Parkin
Icon made by OCHA from www.flaticon.com under CC BY 3.0 license; adapted by Marny K. Parkin

ISBN 978-1-947966-15-4

Printed in the United States of America

In memory of my late father Joseph Mandrick, who endured the horrors of war and still did his best to make life "just a bowl of cherries" for his wife and only daughter. The thought of his sacrifice and courage still leaves me breathless.

Contents

Chapter One

Dementia Dolls

"IF YOU WANT TO CRY, I'LL GIVE YOU SOMETHING TO CRY about!" my mother said in frustration at least a million times during my childhood.

It wasn't until recently that she made good on her promise.

"Why don't you want a doll?" my mother asked as her *de rigueur* high heels clattered across the linoleum floor of the Sears department store in Union City, New Jersey. Back in the day, Sears was *the* destination for all manner of Christmas gifts. Compared with the sprawling malls of today and the ability to get whatever you need through online shopping, Sears seems in retrospect a quaint antiquity—sort of like Matuschek & Company in *The Shop Around the Corner,* one of my favorite Christmas movies. But on that day in 1962, I felt like I was at the center of it all as we passed row upon row of gleaming new dolls—babies with pinkish ivory skin and blue or green eyes, or bigger girl dolls with dimples and blonde banana curls. So much variety!

"I just don't!" I answered. Weeks before, my mother had asked if I would like a baby brother or sister. I had let her know that I would not. The cute baby dolls now represented my possible competition, and I was having none of that.

A four-year-old, hazel-eyed girl with olive skin and a halo of soft curly brown hair, I skipped past the dolls and my mother standing wistfully in front of them. My gaze landed on the stuffed animals and the skyscraper-building kits. I wanted those toys. Most likely I would get them as well as the doll my mother wanted me to have and hold and love. Not just because I was spoiled, either.

The real reason for my mother's generosity went much deeper. Mom was trying to give me the idyllic childhood she had longed for but never had. She was trying to fill a void.

If you asked my mom to describe herself as a young girl in three words, they would be fatherless, fat, and stupid. Mom had a tough time of it growing up. One of her earliest memories was a Christmas morning when she was four years old. My mom, Josephine, and her older sister, Millie, had received the baby dolls they asked for, one for each of them. This was sort of a Christmas miracle, since money was tight. Then Mom's older cousin arrived for a visit and saw the dolls. She demanded one for her daughters to share. "My daughters can share, and your daughters can share," she explained to my grandma Anna, Mom's mother. My grandma Anna, a widow who was beholden to her relatives, took my mom's doll and gave it to her cousin. Mom swears she's never been the same since that horrible incident, and I believe her.

Mom was angry, of course, but never held a grudge against my grandma Anna. Somehow Mom became more demanding of herself. I guess it's possible to go from "I didn't deserve to have my doll taken away" to "I didn't deserve to have my doll." Mom set off on a lifelong course of self-improvement and sacrifice. Mom was and still is admired for being impeccably well-coiffed and well-dressed. Despite sporadic attempts at dieting, she always ended up at the weight most suitable for her large frame. She is not slim, but she is not chubby. She is solid and attractive. Despite her utterances to the contrary, she fills out her clothing nicely. Her height of nearly five feet and her beautiful face compel everyone to want to love her on sight. She is, in a word, adorable.

At five feet seven inches, I tower over Mom. I have unruly hair and a disdain for gussying up. "Is *this* your daughter?" is something Mom has heard many times. To all the world, we appear to be polar opposites. But appearances can be deceiving. I learned self-improvement and sacrifice from the best of teachers. Mom and I throw everything we have at the world. Give us a void of any kind, and we will try to fill it. If there is a lull in conversation, or sadness in someone's eyes, or a situation that seems unfair, we feel it is our sworn duty to step in and make things right. Sometimes our interventions are well-received and successful, and other times they are not. We often say or do the wrong thing, unintentionally, which creates a whole other can of worms. We are described as a "presence." Together and separately, we wonder why we can never sit back and just be. Yet we can't seem to help ourselves. It's exhausting to be us.

"You are your father's daughter" is something Mom always said. I always believed this was true. Now I am not so sure.

I take after my father physically. I have his strong facial features and auburn hair and wide smile. I have his tall and slender frame. And I always felt a kinship with his side of the family, especially since I ended up being raised in close proximity to them. They were a fun and eccentric group, and to be considered one of them was a high honor indeed. I was a jokester and a smart-aleck, and proud of it. When you are basking in the sound of laughter, it is easy to forget about the person who isn't in on the joke, the one lurking in the shadows and reminding everyone that life should be taken more seriously. That would be my mom. And now it's me as well.

For most of my life, I believed that a breezy attitude and a ready smile could get you through everything in life. Then things came crashing down, and I needed my rock. Not my jokester father. But my sensible mother.

God answers your prayers in strange ways. Either that, or He truly does have a sense of humor. He delivered Mom back to me, as a widow with dementia who could no longer live on her own. The three years I spent caring for Mom in my home made me stronger than I thought I could be. It wasn't just the task of caregiving that brought me around. It was having my mother back under the same roof to teach me, support me, and move me forward.

One of the toughest tests of my parents' marriage—and some of the most unnerving yet memorable years of my life— occurred when my grandma Anna moved in with us when I was about to begin high school. During this stressful time, I lost my mother for a little while. She was absorbed in the day-to-day details of caring for her own mom. Over a three-year period, my grandma's physical frailties worsened, and she began crying out in her sleep at night. This was in the late 1970s, when not a lot was known about dementia. A lack of understanding and discussion about the disease left us helpless. I couldn't imagine why my sweet grandmother became a different person once the sun went down. My father couldn't sleep, and my mother—the one who felt the weight of it all—seemed sad and distracted. It made me nervous. I was used to being the center of Mom's universe. I longed for her care and validation. I wanted her to come back.

Then one day, in the midst of all this angst, my mother did something that surprised me. She placed a record on my father's ever-present turntable—*his* domain—and came over to where I stood in the living room.

"We're going to dance the Lindy," she announced. My mother had been quite the accomplished dancer in her day and always expressed surprise that she had married a non-dancer. When she said that I was my father's daughter, she had made clear her suspicions that the non-dancing gene was part of the package. But here she was giving me a chance.

When the music began, my mother twirled and jumped with a grace and athleticism that shocked me. With my hand gripped in hers, I did my best to keep up. I began to laugh, but Mom was dead serious. Determined to get me through this dance. Determined to teach me the steps she had mastered during the halcyon days when she was attending dances and being lauded for her skill. Determined to show me that the world doesn't fall apart just because you are facing a challenge. Determined to demonstrate that, like my dad and other Mandrick relatives, she was capable of showing me a fun time. Determined to show me that when you dance, you forget your troubles.

I was exhilarated and exhausted by the time the song ended, and Mom lifted the phonograph needle up before the next tune began. I was pooped but disappointed. I wanted to give this another shot, and I told her so.

"Maybe another time," she said.

But that dance with my mother never happened again. My Lindy-dancing mother thrilled me with a brief appearance that day when I was fourteen and never came back.

Mom and I are doing another dance now. It is a mother-daughter dance for the ages, and through this ongoing dance we are finally learning to anticipate each other's every move and bend to each other's wills. It's the only way the two of us are going to survive without killing each other.

At the tender age of fifty-eight, I have decided there is a huge advantage to having your parents, but especially your mother, live to an advanced age. My mother and I have had ample opportunity to examine past rifts and misunderstandings and either defend ourselves or apologize. Sometimes both at the same time. I can't tell you what a joy and blessing it is to work with my mother to relive precious memories. At the same time, we have hashed out and let go of the unpleasant ones, the ones that hurt us so long ago but are powerless to touch us anymore.

The gift of time has brought us to a new level of understanding. We get each other.

Here is what I now know for sure about my mother. At pretty much two-thirds of my height, and with her frailty becoming more apparent and her dementia worsening, my mother is still going to lead. I will dance to her tune even when I don't feel like it. She does what she feels is right and good about 99.9 percent of the time. She is trustworthy.

Here is what my mother knows for sure about me. I will sometimes behave selfishly and capriciously and I will get upset about small things that shouldn't matter. But I will never lose my temper with her and I will be pleasant about ninety-five percent of the time. If I am unpleasant, it is because I have once again placed myself in the unfortunate position of doing too much for too many. My biggest goal in life is to take care of my family and friends and keep them safe. I, too, am trustworthy.

A few months after my mother moved in with us, I attempted to entertain her by dancing energetically to the opening theme of one of her favorite TV shows, *Wheel of Fortune*. I have always enjoyed making up goofy moves to television theme songs, but I amped up this activity when my mother became the fifth member of our household.

"I'm a good dancer, right, Ma?" I laughed as she sat on the sofa nearby. She forced a smile but I could tell she was sort of horrified. But still, any port in a storm, right? I was not accustomed to staying in the house and watching TV night after night. The routine was wearing on my husband and me. I was attempting to relieve my boredom and stress and wanted to believe that some part of my mother appreciated the spectacle.

Later on that evening, my daughter Veronica approached me with information. "Sometimes when you dance, Grammy rolls her eyes at you when she knows you're not looking," she said.

I smiled because this was what I suspected. Deep down I was a little hurt, and my daughter looked hurt for me. "I sort of figured as much, and it's okay," I said as she looked doubtful. "It's really fine," I said again to reassure her. She sighed and walked away.

And it *was* fine. Mom had never made a secret of the fact that she did not consider me to be a good dancer. You can add singing to the list as well. Yes, it used to frustrate me and make me feel sad. But like I said, water under the bridge. And if it made my mother feel good to share an inside joke with my daughter, even in the form of a jab at my dancing, that was okay by me. Mom had fallen far in the past few years. She'd lost her husband. She'd lost her independence. She'd lost her purpose. And, finally, she'd lost some of her luster.

I had hoped that a sort of excitement would come over my family upon Mom's arrival. Instead, logistics took over.

"Is it safe for Mom to walk in the hallway to the bathroom?"

"Looks like she's going to need help getting up and down the stairs!"

"She likes to see the TV during dinner, let her sit in Veronica's chair!"

Faced with the task of keeping my mom safe and well-cared for, we all felt drained. Resentment seeped in. I can recall feeling powerless to stop it and hoping Mom didn't notice. On occasion, though, I did see guilt and sadness in her eyes. I saw it that evening, when we were watching TV. All of us seemed glum. So I tried to fix the situation by doing what we used to do best, together.

My display wasn't as much about the dancing as it was about validating her existence by carrying on our hallowed tradition.

The tradition of attempting to fill a void.

Chapter Two

Heat Wave

IT WAS GREAT UNTIL IT WASN'T.

I was on a playground in Fair Haven in 2002 with my two children and our new friends when I received the phone call from Mom. Dad had fallen while waiting for her to finish shopping in the local food store. He had already driven her to church and picked her up on a blazingly hot day. The fall had resulted in action by good Samaritans and an ambulance ride to the hospital with Mom by his side. The end result was a diagnosis of an irregular heartbeat and the insertion of a pacemaker. Shortly after this, he was diagnosed with wet macular degeneration. Almost all of his eyesight was gone, save for what he could see out of the corners of his brilliant blue eyes.

Within months they had sold their home, collecting (with our help) whatever they wanted or needed from the attic and elsewhere and leaving the rest for the neighbor who bought their house to deal with. They moved to a rental in the same Long Branch complex as my mother's sister Millie and bought new furniture for the kitchen and living room. I had just been diagnosed with Lyme disease and was often feeling bone tired. My mother offered to let me off the hook and find someone else to help her. But I insisted on being in charge of the move. Even now, I question this decision on my part. The move was tough on all of us, but it was torture for me. Part of my discomfort lay with the exhaustion I felt at that time. And part of it was due to the fact that my freedom was over.

At first I had felt guilty about my family's move to Fair Haven in August 2000. It was an hour farther from my parents than our former town of Union. I knew my parents couldn't make the hour-and-a-half trip to see me, and my trips to visit them would be less frequent. But after a little while, I found the distance sort of refreshing. It wasn't exactly a case of out of sight, out of mind, but it was a welcome respite. I thought about them often, but my dad's sister Betty lived in an apartment complex less than two blocks from them, and they seemed content. Mom discovered that she had a lot in common with Aunt Betty, and they food shopped together and shared evening visits.

The summer of 2002 brought an end not only to my contentment, but to theirs as well.

What followed the move was a combination of "Breaking Up [with your house] Is Hard to Do" (Mom and Dad) and "No good deed goes unpunished" (me).

Mom had a litany of complaints:

"That stuff in the attic was valuable; it's a shame that we left it there."

"I miss Aunt Betty so much."

"Nothing happens around here; it's boring."

As Mom uttered this final one yet again, I had to counterpoint. "What are you waiting for, some crime?"

But the zingers kept on coming, and Mom was more than happy to be Dad's mouthpiece as well.

"Dad misses his deck."

"Dad misses his model trains."

"Dad misses his sister Betty."

Aunt Betty had been a bright spot in our lives and a harbinger of fun during my parents' last years in their home at Sixty-Eight Overlook. During a time when my parents really should have been moving on from home ownership, Aunt Betty single-handedly made it possible for them to stay. She was, in a word, amazing.

My dad's youngest sister, Aunt Betty had rented an apartment just blocks from my parents in late 1986 after losing her husband Halsey to cancer. She arrived also to help care for my aunt Bernice, who passed away from cancer soon after Halsey did. After my husband John and I moved forty minutes away to our first home in Union, Aunt Betty and my mom got to know one another much better. They became close friends and confidantes as well as sisters-in-law. In the late 1990s, when she was in her seventies, Aunt Betty hosted me during overnight stays when I brought my young children to visit. Greg and Veronica stayed with my parents while I stayed with my aunt, waking up to home-cooked breakfasts that would make Guy Fieri want to pull up a chair and stay a while.

Aunt Betty enlightened me about my father's wartime experiences and the changes that became apparent after his return home. My dad's enduring sadness, something my mother and I had never discussed, was one of the topics that Aunt Betty and I touched upon during those wonderful evenings when we sat in her living room with cups of tea. We chatted as the trucks on the nearby New Jersey Turnpike hummed in the distance.

Aunt Betty's apartment, decorated in soothing pastel tones, felt even more intimate and comfortable than her lovely former home in Emerson. It had been during a family gathering there, in the summer of 1971 when I was thirteen, that I learned something significant about my father's wartime experience. Before we arrived, my mom mentioned that an old friend of my dad's named Bob would be there.

"I fought with him in the war," Dad added simply.

When I met Bob, he told me something that surprised me. "Your father saved my life," he said. Bob explained that my father had urged him into a foxhole and saved him from being strafed by bullets from an enemy plane. I had heard a similar story a few years before from my father, who said that he was sitting in a field playing poker with his buddies when he got a "sixth sense" that enemy planes were approaching. He urged all of his friends to get into the foxhole with him. Almost all of them told Dad he was crazy. Dad had told me they teased him about his "vision" instead of listening to him and surviving. But he never told me about Bob.

Bob, a very kind and gentle man, explained that he was the only one who put down his cards and climbed into the foxhole with Dad. That decision, which I suspect may have been made because Bob felt sorry for my dad, saved his life. And *that*, I realized years later, was what made Dad sad after the war. Yes, he had saved Bob. But the rest of the soldiers, including one who had attended high school in Jersey City with him, had died. Dad's melancholy wasn't the result of everything he had been through, which included fighting on the front lines under General Patton and taking part in fierce and famous battles such as Anzio. And it wasn't what he'd lost, which included his longtime girlfriend when she moved on.

What made him sad was thinking about the men he could not save, in that situation and so many others that I learned about in dribs and drabs. (One story involved a German soldier who "disappeared" from a POW camp after disobeying an order from a group of U.S. soldiers from the South. Handed a shovel and ordered to dig a hole, the German soldier mistakenly believed he was digging his own grave. Unable to speak English, he showed photos of his family in desperation and dropped his shovel. Shortly thereafter he was driven away by the group of Southern soldiers and never seen again. My father was convinced that the German soldier had suffered a grisly death, and his heart broke for him.)

As my father reached his nineties, he began to share more of his wartime experiences with me. Before then, it had been too painful.

It was my aunt Betty who filled in the blanks for me before that point, and I was extremely grateful. During one of our heart-to-hearts in her apartment, Aunt Betty showed me a photo of my father as a teenager. I insisted it couldn't be him, because he was smiling widely and there was a light in his eyes.

"Oh, it's your father all right," Aunt Betty replied.

I looked at the photo again, and for the first time I felt my heartstrings tugged by the plight of the happy young man who had left Jersey City as a twenty-four-year-old and had his life changed forever by the horrors of war. For years I had harbored resentment over my dad's anxiety and his sometimes dark moods, partly because they interfered with my own ability to be joyful. I was a selfish, silly young girl. With Aunt Betty's help, I finally got a grip on how much perseverance and faith it took for my father to build a life after the war.

In Aunt Betty, I found solace and validation. More importantly, my mother found the best friend she had always wanted. Having grown up in the shadow of her more popular sister Millie—bright, slim, quick-witted, and well-spoken—my mother felt like a runner-up for most of her life. She had shared her friends with Aunt Millie, an avid letter writer who kept in touch with them years later. They returned the favor.

"Have you heard the latest about Alice?" Aunt Millie would say, and my mother would shake her head and blush. Aunt Millie would fill her in, kindly, but I could see that my mother felt slighted. My mother was not a good speller and therefore only sent greeting cards.

But with Aunt Betty, my mother began to shine again. She was the co-star of her own friendship show.

I knew I broke Aunt Betty's heart by moving my parents away a few years later in 2002, but I felt I had no choice. With my father almost blind and with heart issues, I figured there was no way they could live on their own any longer, even with Aunt

Betty's help. She, too, was in her eighties, although with her solid frame and glowing skin and sprightly manner, she showed few signs of aging.

But had I made a mistake? Perhaps I acted hastily. Perhaps with Aunt Betty making regular food runs and providing companionship for Mom, I could have sucked it up and made weekly trips up from the shore to do some laundry and housecleaning for my parents. Maybe I could have hired a lawn service for the large and shaded backyard that my dad enjoyed so much. Perhaps I could have sacrificed one weekend a month to tend to their needs and given up my sometimes too-active social life and missed a few of my kids' activities. I could have helped Aunt Betty out as well, repaying her for all of the time and effort she gave for my parents' comfort. I was filled with self-doubt and even self-loathing during my parents' settling in years. In my state of confusion and regret, Mom's complaints sounded like nails on a chalkboard.

I tried to let all of it roll off my shoulders, but it was difficult. I felt like I'd had the rug pulled out from under me. With Dad no longer driving, I was the chauffeur. My parents did try their best to walk when they could. But the wind off the ocean during the winter could be unforgivingly strong and cold. What kind of person would let their elderly parents walk to the food store in a squall? Okay, maybe I would. No, I wouldn't. I'm just kidding. After all, what would happen if people found out? Anyway, I was the wintertime food shopper. And I hated pretty much every minute of it.

I still grimace about the time I went food shopping for my parents and was carrying a store-baked chicken in a plastic bag back to their apartment. A fierce gust of frigid wind ripped the bag from my hand, and the measly chicken flew into the air, escaping from its yellow plastic bag. It landed upright at least ten feet away directly in front of a young resident of the apartment complex, most likely a student at nearby Monmouth University. He picked it up and appeared pleasantly surprised, as though instead of sending manna from the heavens God was now delivering cooked chickens.

"That's my chicken!" I yelled, trying to be heard above the gale force winds pelting my face with freezing cold sea spray. In my bright yellow squall jacket, I am pretty sure I looked like the Gorton's Fisherman. The young man seemed amused, either by the chicken or me. He walked over, smiled, and handed over the prized chicken. I thanked him and headed into the warmth of my parents' apartment.

A few days later, my mother answered a knock on her door to find the same young man standing on the stoop. He asked if he could pick anything up for her at the grocery store. She resisted, not wanting to trouble him. He insisted, and she relented and gave him a short list. This went on every week until he moved out a few months later. Score one for Long Branch. Yep, Mom and Dad, *that's* how we do it at the shore.

Mom and Dad finally came to realize what everyone else "down the shore" seemed to know. Life is more relaxed after you cross over the Driscoll Bridge spanning the Raritan River, leaving Woodbridge and entering Sayreville. And even better, in Dad's opinion anyway, a bus to Atlantic City ran regularly and stopped just a few blocks from their apartment. Of course, they both still worried about running out of money (Mom) and running me ragged (Dad). As it turns out, both worries were valid, although I sure did get sick of hearing about them.

The truth is, I had problems of my own during my parents' Long Branch years. Big ones.

In 2002, my husband John lost his job when he refused to relocate to Georgia. We muddled through, with John running a one-person consulting operation and working odd jobs for my cousin and our friend Tom—both of whom owned small businesses in the local area. By the time John was hired for a full-time job in New Jersey, we had been living off our credit cards and were in a pinch financially. But a few years after that, in 2007, we learned that John required open heart surgery to repair a leaking valve. He was fifty years old.

My mother offered to watch our children during the surgery and recovery. I planned to stay in a hotel room for relatives of patients on the hospital premises for three days. Thinking that it would be too hard on my aging parents to walk my children to the nearby school and keep track of pickups and drop-offs for after-school activities, I declined Mom's offer. I could tell she was upset, and I finally understood what it must be like for them—to be the parent who needs parenting instead of the parent who can help out with the kids. It represented a switch in roles and a turning point in our relationship.

John's surgery was successful, and no one was more relieved than I. There was more to this than met the eye. A few months earlier, when we had no idea that John's heart was struggling, we had planned a Father's Day outing for Mom, Dad, John, me, and our two children. To John's dismay, my mother nixed the idea of a trip to John's favorite all-you-can-eat buffet.

"Daddy hates it there," she said as if that settled the matter. I suspected that it was *Mom* who hated it there. But for some reason I didn't argue. There was an off chance that Mom was lying, but there was also an off chance that she was telling the truth. Mom had a way of bending facts to meet her needs, and I had grown accustomed to it. I was aggravated, for sure—I liked the buffet, and it was an inexpensive option—but for some reason I didn't have the strength to argue or to hear her complaints afterward. I agreed to the change of venue, which my mom had decided would be the local diner.

John, meanwhile, was livid. He, too, suspected this was Mom's doing. He pulled me aside and, glancing at Dad, said, "The man will most likely outlive me!"

Boy, did those words ever come back to haunt me. *Don't let it happen, don't let it happen.* That was all I could think as we made it through those worrisome days leading up to surgery.

Many weeks later, the children and John and I celebrated John's recovery by visiting the buffet. John piled his plate high with food, and the kids enjoyed the machine dispensing soft ice cream and the fish swimming in the giant tank built into a wall. I enjoyed the place, but not as much as I had on previous visits. I didn't go for my usual endless desserts, and I cut down on the fried entrées that had been my favorite. Mom had ruined it for me on her and Dad's last visit there with us almost a year before.

"Mary Ann, did you notice how many of the people here are fat?" she demanded as we sat in our booth waiting for John and the kids to finish their first round of food-gathering. "Have you *seen* them?"

I looked. I saw. I sighed.

This woman will be the death of me, I thought.

And not for the first time.

Chapter Three

It All Started with
an Iron in the Oven

ON MY GOOD DAYS WHEN MOM LIVED WITH ME, I FELT productive and inspired. I felt like a hero.

On my bad days, I felt like my family and I were facing a deplorable situation that was the result of bad decisions I had made. I felt like a dope.

If there was a middle ground, I couldn't find it.

I never saw this coming, the dementia. I wish there were a better word for it, not related to "demented." That word always calls to mind a wild-eyed man holding a cleaver, or Jack Nicholson in *The Shining*.

I do recall the actor David Hyde Pierce trying to raise public awareness about Alzheimer's disease years ago. While I appreciated his earnestness, I concluded, like so many people, that Alzheimer's would not touch my family and I needn't worry about it. Both of my parents were as sharp as tacks. Too sharp, in fact. Nothing got past them! Even just a few years before my mom's dementia diagnosis, I listened to the stories of friends struggling with their parents. There were dads taking the car keys and driving down the road and an Amber Alert being issued, or moms acting up and screaming during their daughters' visits to the assisted living facility. While I sympathized, I simply could not relate. I thought this could never happen to me. It was as though they were describing some eventful trip to a foreign land that I had no intention of visiting. And so I stared, blank-faced, instead of giving them the compassion or encouragement they so badly needed.

Now these same people are bolstering me up during my toughest time with my mother. My lack of understanding and empathy has, apparently, been forgiven by these kind friends. And I am chastened.

But back to Mom. She always had a sort of quirky personality. I guess you could say that about anyone, so I will be specific. I think she would be best characterized as sort of ODD, as in oppositional defiant disorder. As a toddler, she was so rough on my widowed grandmother that a priest was called in to rid her of demons. I never asked Mom how that went. Because I knew. That priest had not gotten the job done.

My mother had a will of iron, paired with an angelic face and a fair amount of charisma. She was a good girl, for sure, but with a mind of her own. She was well versed in pretending to do exactly what you were asking, but she always had her own agenda.

I was in my thirties before my sharp-eyed sister-in-law Robin alerted me to this fact. I was trying to host my yearly Thanksgiving dinner for a crowd, and despite the fact that my mother and Robin were doing their best to help me, some of the things I was asking for were not getting done. It was frustrating and stressful.

Robin pulled me aside, and I could see that all-too-familiar steely sense of purpose in her eyes. Unlike me, Robin is nobody's fool. I am blessed to have her in my life to give me much-needed perspective.

"Have you noticed that when you ask your mom to do something, she does what she wants to instead?" she asked.

"Oh gosh," I said, and glanced over to see Mom putting the plates out on the table. Moments before, I had asked her to fill the ice buckets and set out the silver. Defiant? Confused? What my mother, then in her late sixties, was experiencing at that given moment was anybody's guess. Robin had been kind to point out what was happening. She adored my mom, but she knew I was feeling overwhelmed by entertaining, despite Mom's help. Now I realized it was partly because of Mom's help.

Until Robin spoke up, I had thought that perhaps I was losing *my* mind. Although it happened many years ago, I still recall how I felt in that moment. Enlightened. Somewhat empowered. And weary. Very weary. I am always surprised when people refer to me as "a presence." I really don't think I am. But perhaps that is because I pale in comparison with "Hurricane Josephine." Yes, Mom can appear calm in the eye of the storm. And that's because she is usually the one who created it in the first place.

This was why the prospect of moving my mom in to live with us gave me a serious case of the frights. After Dad passed away, we would make offhand offers to move her in. And when she demurred, either saying she was fine or didn't want to disrupt our household, I would quickly change the subject. I was being a chicken, really, and in retrospect I should have insisted. And so Mom, who had nursed Dad through prostate cancer on her own in their apartment, was now living alone.

Then one evening, when we were visiting Mom a full year after my Dad had passed, a lightbulb turned on in my head.

Wait, that's wrong. A lightbulb turned on in my mother's oven, when she opened the oven door. And there it was.

Her iron.

"Grammy, what is your iron doing in the oven?" my daughter asked.

My mother furrowed her brows. "Why? Where else would it be?" Mom answered.

"In the utility closet?" I asked, my heart racing.

"Why would I put in in there?" she said, confused. With her Hudson County accent, "there" sounded like "they-ah."

John and I looked at each other in alarm. Not three weeks later, Mom was set up in our house in Greg's former upstairs bedroom. It was tiny but cute, just like her, and when I managed to find an inexpensive wardrobe/closet that was just Mom's height, I took it as a good sign.

After tossing a seemingly endless number of black bags filled with all manner of memorabilia into the dumpster at Mom's complex, we said our last goodbye to the apartment and to my mother's "landlords": the housing staff at Monmouth University, which had bought the former Diplomat Apartments for student use.

I braced myself for a new adventure as we said our sad final goodbyes to the apartment. The last thing I remember seeing was a row of pencil lines on the frame of my parents' utility closet charting our children's growth.

I took a walk to the nearby ocean and stood on the beach. And there it was. The sensation that had been making itself known and I had studiously ignored. It wasn't the salty breeze or the sunlight bouncing off a nearby sailboat in glints and throwing specks of golden light into my eyes.

It was the sand. It was the sand shifting under my feet.

Chapter Four

Circling the Wagons

WHEN MOM FIRST BEGAN LIVING WITH US, A TYPICAL workday phone conversation between my husband and me might have gone like this:

Me: I decided that I will make pepper steak for dinner tonight.

John: Pepper steak? That is awesome. I was thinking that you should make pepper steak.

Me: Okay, good! Yes, I am really excited about the pepper steak.

John: Me, too!

We don't get this excited about pepper steak. We were both employing our coping mechanism of forced cheerfulness. John and I had been suffering from mild depression since our young birds had flown the nest for college and the old bird had taken up residence. I was able to admit it to close friends, but John wouldn't admit it to anyone, not even himself. He keeps his secrets well.

"Let's circle the wagons," he will say when an embarrassment or hardship befalls us. I always nod, as if I am on board with this idea of handling our problem by keeping our spirits up and putting on a game face for the rest of the world.

Meanwhile, I'm ready to buy paint for a big sign that says, "We need help." I am always optimistic that somehow someone will throw us a lifeline. John is always optimistic that with enough prayer and good intentions and reflection, our unspoken problems will somehow solve themselves. See? We're both optimists.

Our optimism really blew up in our faces when we decided to move Mom into our home.

"It will be fine," we told ourselves. And I believed this more than John did. Mom would be great company for me while I worked from home, and we would enjoy watching evening TV shows together. Surely she could manage to stay alone for an evening, or even an extended period of time, if we left enough food and beverages in the refrigerator for her.

But the Mom who entered our home was not the same Mom who had cared for Dad. Something had changed. The Mom we knew, who was "large and in charge," was suddenly content to hand me the reins. Relieved, actually. The woman who John called "the Mighty Mite" was asking me to make all of her decisions.

"It's up to you," she announced when we asked what she wanted for dinner the day we moved her in. "Whatever you want, that's what I'll have."

This from the woman who had had a hissy fit just a few years before when I insisted that she and Dad accompany us on a trip to Five Guys Burgers.

"Daddy likes hot dogs," she said.

"They'll have hot dogs there," I said hopefully.

They did. But no sauerkraut. Mom, incensed by this omission, pointed to the fry cooks behind the glass.

"Are those the five guys?" she asked.

Before I could answer, she walked over and demanded to know why they did not serve sauerkraut with their hot dogs. Every one of those five guys apologized.

But headstrong Mom had been replaced by someone a lot less with it. At first we thought Mom was deferring to us because we were the homeowners. But the questions and confusion never abated. Mom still had her high standards, though. She made that obvious during a family dinner within the first few days of her arrival.

"Am I spreading this butter around?" she asked when I handed her a slice of Italian bread with a large pat of butter resting squarely in the middle.

"Yes," I said, fetching her a butter knife. My own family was resigned to my somewhat haphazard offerings at dinnertime and other meals. A perfectionist I was not. Not nearly. Mom was another ball of wax entirely. This was going to be one of many challenges.

"I can dust that cabinet later," she said, looking at the film atop the nearby dining room buffet just a few minutes after she had spread the butter ever so carefully to the edges of the Italian bread.

"Okay," I said, hoping she would forget. She did. She began forgetting more and more.

After a few weeks, John became puzzled and frustrated. And I was scared to death. I took frequent walks so John and the kids wouldn't see me crying. I stopped taking daily showers and dressed in sweatpants and my trusted zippered fleece, hunter green and highly unattractive. I always tried to pick as much of the lint off it as I could.

I recall startling an acquaintance at the local grocery store. "I almost didn't recognize you," she said honestly, with a fleeting concern in her eyes before she changed the subject.

She was a Board of Education member and was accustomed to the Mary Ann who showed up to cover school events as a freelance press release writer, sporting a full face of makeup and always wearing slacks and a blouse. I am sure she expected at the very least blue jeans and washed hair and lip gloss. My lowered standards weren't just for in-home use any longer. I thought about all the Acme cashiers who had been subjected to my makeup-free face and coffee breath.

"Well, this was sort of like buying a used car," John said one morning when I began crying at the breakfast table while Mom was sleeping. "We didn't really know what was under the hood."

I agreed, but I still thought Mom was driving me crazy on purpose. I had convinced myself Mom had changed her mind about being large and in charge. She was deferring to me since she was now living in my home.

What I didn't know, and would not figure out for nearly half a year, was that the issue wasn't that Mom had changed her mind.

It was that her mind had changed Mom.

Chapter Five

Doctor Who?

"WHAT YEAR IS IT, JOSEPHINE?"

"I don't know. Mary Ann, what year is it?"

"No, Josephine, I need you to answer."

"2000-something."

"It's 2014, Mom!" I blurted out. The doctor rolled her eyes and continued her line of questioning.

"Very good. Now, Josephine, who is our president?"

"I don't know. Mary Ann, who is our president?"

"No, Josephine, I need you to answer."

"I am not sure, but I know it's not Nixon."

We were facing yet another doctor, this one a neurologist Mom had seen during a recent hospital stay. Mom had fallen almost halfway down the stairs leading to her bedroom and ended up sprawled on a hardwood landing. This happened a little less than a year after she moved in with us.

"One fall, and it's all over," Uncle Paul had proclaimed repeatedly in his sixties. He died in his seventies from a fall that broke his hip. I had sworn that I would never let my mom fall while she was living in my home.

I praised God for the fact that no bones had been broken, partly because I felt horribly guilty. I'd sent Mom back upstairs to wash her hands after breakfast, even though she looked off. I was standing on the landing and keeping track of her progress when she suddenly seized up and pitched backward. I tried to catch her and then, realizing it was fruitless, backed up and just let her roll down the stairs.

Mom has big bones. She came down those stairs like a boulder. Flailing my Olive Oyl arms in an attempt to do God knows what, I didn't manage to break her fall in the least.

This episode resulted in a free ride in an ambulance and a three-day hospital stay with scans of her heart and brain. The brain scan showed damage had occurred to the frontal lobe, not necessarily as a result of the fall but most likely from another diagnosis concerning her heart. An echocardiogram showed that Mom had a growth on her mitral valve. Eerily enough, this growth had "arms" that loosened and tightened but posed no immediate threat to her heart function. The growth on my mother's heart was cutting off oxygen to her brain when it flexed its muscles, so to speak, and was most likely the cause of her blackout. I was told that the growth was extremely rare and not cancerous. At Mom's age, surgery was out of the question. The growth would probably not affect her life span, although it could result in another episode.

I tried to get more answers about how this growth could be affecting her brain function. When I questioned the cardiologist, she suggested I set up an office visit with the neurologist who had seen Mom in the hospital. Upon Mom's discharge, I still did not have a diagnosis of dementia. Caregivers are expected to do so much with so little information. It's a problem that I don't think will be solved any time soon.

Shortly after Mom was released from the hospital, I "fired" the general practitioner she had seen for years and hired the GP who had seen her in the hospital. I liked his quiet manner and that he was not pushing me to "do more" to "solve" what was happening with Mom. Mom's former GP had repeatedly suggested that Mom's need for long naps was a result of her being bored and depressed, and she told me to "try and figure out some fun activities for the two of you."

The frustration and guilt I felt at the end of that statement was suffocating.

Mom's new GP didn't blink an eye when, during our first post-hospital office visit, I told him about her long naps. And he didn't mince words when I asked him point-blank if my mom had dementia.

"It appears that she's in the beginning stages," he said, and I almost fell off the chair.

The beginning? I thought. Holy shnikies, how much worse is it going to get?

Doing my best Lady Gaga impersonation, I put on a poker face. "Do you think I should follow up with the cardiologist and the neurologist she saw in the hospital?"

"Yes, that would be a good idea," he answered, to my dismay. Mom had never been seen by specialists, and I dreaded the additional office visits.

Long story short, the cardiologist was a bust. For a year I endured her surly office staff and messed-up communications, which resulted in my dragging Mom out on a nasty February day when her scheduled EKG had been canceled and no one bothered to phone and tell me.

A few weeks later I received no insight into the growth rate of the intruder on Mom's valve. The cardiologist pronounced the EKG, which we had been able to reschedule, as "unreadable." I turned to a friend who had cared for her own mom and her mother-in-law for years. I was looking for absolution. She gave it.

"Ditch the heart doctor, and don't worry about it," she said. "I've ditched a lot of specialists."

And that was it. I hesitated to tell Mom's primary doctor about my decision. But to my relief, he let me off the hook as well.

"I check her heart regularly, so don't worry."

I also dumped the neurologist. She sent us home after that initial visit with no clear answer, a scheduled follow-up visit (so we could look forward to losing yet another hour of our lives in her waiting areas), and a prescription. I dutifully filled the prescription and began administering the medication to my mom and hoping for the best, although I wasn't quite sure what "the best" would entail. I certainly did not expect a miracle, but I hoped for improvement.

I got neither. Even worse, the drug had a negative effect on Mom's appetite almost immediately. "She's eating well, God bless her," was something positive I used to say when pressed for news on Mom's health and well-being. Now the one bright spot had been taken away by this drug. Mom pushed her plate aside three days in a row.

Feeling hopeful but embarrassed, I posted a photo of the bottle of pills on social media. "Has anyone had experience with the drug Namenda? My mother has dementia and it was prescribed." My mother has dementia. *My mother has dementia.* This was the first time I had admitted it in public, and I did not know what to expect. After hitting the button to post publicly, I had such a fright I thought that my hair might be standing on end.

To my relief, a few comments soon appeared, and the majority of them validated my concern and observation. Then another message—this one from a friend whose grandmother had become anorexic after using Namenda for a period of time—arrived in my private messenger inbox. I was grateful for my friend's honesty. But I was not myself at that time, and I became concerned about how my friend had used a private message in order to not publicly out her relative, as I just had.

Although I was emboldened by the responses—an overwhelming thumbs down for Namenda—I was terrified by the possibility that I had shamed my own mother. I spent a restless night thinking about what I had done, and many days after that feeling I had let Mom down in a very public way.

Sometimes the most painful incidents provide the best lessons, and here is what I took away from this one. First of all, don't ever think you know the motive behind someone else's actions. You don't. Second, don't feel badly about asking for help when you need it. Mom would have understood my concern and my decision to ask a very public question. She felt badly about me being an only child and having to care for her and Dad on my own. Finally, diseases like dementia and anorexia are not shameful. That doesn't mean that everyone wants their struggles made public. But Mom, who always wanted to provide a helping hand no matter what the cost, would understand my need to share her story.

The Facebook incident initially chastened but eventually emboldened me. I now use the word *dementia* with abandon. Each time I say or write it, I feel like I am diminishing its power. Dementia is not shameful.

Dementia should not be kept secret. I say it loud. Dementia. Dementia. DEMENTIA. I have become an unstoppable force.

Hmm. Sounds like someone I know.

Chapter Six

Roll It Up and Run!

I ARRIVED AT OUR LOCAL GRAMMAR SCHOOL ONE DAY AND saw something incredible: a swarm of second-grade parents hovering over their children and their poster projects with umbrellas as they entered the school. Even though it was raining hard, this was surprising because the school's principal had a strict rule due to space limitations: on-street parking was temporary, for drop-off only. I had rarely seen a parent set foot on the curb, never mind make it past the flagpole, during drop-off. It was the school's principal, not the parents, who escorted students out of the car. Yet these parents had double-parked their cars and actually stepped out of them into the air surrounding the school, in defiance of the long-standing rule.

Being a rule-follower, I had managed to find a slot in the drop-off lane with Veronica and Greg in the car. I had no thoughts of removing them from the vehicle nor walking them into the building, even though second-grader Greg had created a poster project. I knew how things went down. The principal would open the door, and my obedient kids would bound out of the car and up the path. Both Veronica, a first-grader, and Greg were taking in the scene before them, and I am sure that they were both hoping I would reach for an umbrella and defy the "parents don't exit the car, the students do" rule. They were hoping I would escort them and Greg's poster into the building raindrop-free, as the other parents were.

In addition to my "good girls obey the rules" attitude, the other issue preventing this dream come true was that I had no umbrella at hand. Hadn't I noticed that it was raining when we left the house? Why hadn't I grabbed an umbrella? I am not detail-oriented, but I knew this inaction veered past that and placed me firmly in bad-mom territory. I did manage to locate a rubber band in my car's cup holder. I handed it to Greg. "Roll it up and run!" I instructed Greg as his sympathetic sister looked on wide-eyed.

Greg managed to do just that with his poster, and he and Veronica bravely exited the car. The two of them got slammed with raindrops before making it to the school entrance. The last thing I saw as they entered the doorway was Veronica gazing back at me.

"Dang!" I said aloud.

"Please move along!" the principal told me.

I did.

I felt horrible, as though I wasn't up to snuff, and now even my kids knew it. Well, maybe they knew it already. Feeling glum, I decided that it would be a good idea to head to my parents' apartment in Long Branch to share my story with them. I hoped they would be of comfort and not side with the umbrella faction. I was relieved by their reaction.

"What's the big deal?" my mom said. "A couple of raindrops, are you kidding?"

My father was more direct. "Those parents are dopes," he said, and told my mother to make me a cup of tea.

Case closed. Whether it was the tea or the usual no-nonsense delivery from my dad, I felt better; I felt like a little girl being comforted again. I regained my composure, as I so often did when compelled by my parents to do so.

Fast-forward to 2014. I was once again feeling not up to snuff, and this time I couldn't race over to my parents' apartment for tea and sympathy. I didn't know where to turn until I realized there was a plan B. It involved my friend Jules, who had been my partner in crime for many years.

I arrived at Jules's home, which was decorated in a modern and chic yet comforting way that reflected her personality. I sat on her brown leather sofa and basked in the glow of diffused lighting as it warmed the white walls of her living room. I felt like I was in a sanctuary, a safe place. I could tell Jules anything, and I trusted her. We went way back. Our sons met in second grade and had become fast friends. Jules and I were somewhat well-known for following our sons around in her white Toyota RAV4 with a supply of toilet paper on Mischief Night.

"Do ya'll need more?" Jules had said repeatedly in her Texas twang that evening between puffs of her slim lady's cigar as our sons papered local trees. In retrospect, perhaps it wasn't the best idea. But, like most everything Jules and I did, it was freeing and fun.

I decided to begin the conversation on a light note. Since Jules no longer lived in Fair Haven, I brought her up to date on how many expensive late-model cars I had seen lately in town, and how many smaller homes were being torn down to make way for much larger ones. "It's like some of these people think money can buy happiness," I said.

Jules took this in for a moment and responded thoughtfully. "You know, you and I bought into that stuff somewhat as well," she said.

It took a minute for this to sink in. Jules had been raised in a small town in Texas, and I had lived in blue-collar towns during my childhood. Our friendship was based, I believed, on the fact that we were both outsiders and free thinkers. Now she was telling me otherwise, and just when I needed her to make me feel better about myself. Jules said nothing as I processed what she had said. This was wise, because I was able to recall what I'd said more than once when I felt that my kids were mistreated by friends, classmates, teachers, or coaches: "We pay a fortune to live here, and I'm dealing with *this*?" Once again, Jules was right.

Something inside me shook loose at Jules's statement. I decided to confess what I had told no one else. I confided that I was feeling like an onlooker in my own life, unable to connect with people and places and events. It felt like punishment, I added for good measure. Jules took a drag of her lady's cigar and exhaled before making her pronouncement.

"You're not being punished, you're being taught," she said. "If you've lost your connection, it's your own fault. You need to take yourself down a notch. A good start would be walking around in the grass in your bare feet to renew your connection to the earth."

Jules has some unconventional beliefs, and so do I. And none is stronger than our belief in one another. I trusted her advice.

I went home that night and, after Mom was asleep, I did as I was told. It was a short walk, just around my patio. The cool grass tickled my feet, and I took in a deep breath as I tried not to laugh. Amazingly, I felt better. And then I thought about a nightmare I'd had the night before Mom moved in.

In the nightmare, I found myself at the bottom of a deep pit. I was shocked and looked up expectantly, hoping someone would be there to throw me a rope. With no one in sight, I leaned against the wall of the pit in defeat. When I felt the earth against my back, I turned around to claw at it and let it run through my fingers. The feeling of fright abated, and a sense of being at one with the earth took over. I once again felt aware and as though I were being placed, one molecule at a time, back into my body.

Trudging around my patio that night, I was able to finally get at the wisdom delivered in that nightmare. I ended up at the bottom of that pit well in advance of Mom's arrival. I had lost my way. Mom's arrival had almost nothing to do with me hitting rock bottom, and almost everything to do with finding myself again. I needed to let go of my inflated ego and ask for help. I needed friends with ropes.

And where were those friends when I needed them?

Everywhere, as it turned out.

Chapter Seven

Lifelines

MY GRANDMA ANNA WAS A WISE WOMAN OF GREAT FAITH. And something she knew and taught me was this: God will listen when no one else will and point you in the right direction. But taking that first step is up to you.

In the early 1970s, my mom worked for Fabergé cosmetics company on the assembly line. They had a popular TV advertisement in which a model said, "I told a friend about Fabergé Organics Shampoo, and then she told two friends, and so on and so on." Eventually the TV screen was filled with a montage of beautiful women washing their hair.

That TV commercial was what came to mind after I finally took that first step.

On Thanksgiving Day in 2014, after Mom had moved in, John and I were encouraged by my brother-in-law Jim to start blogging. Jim is always up on the latest technology, and he was very positive about the benefits of blogging. John began immediately, creating a website about New Jersey connections to the entertainment industry. I did not take action until a full year later, when John encouraged me to attend a writing workshop at a local community college. Blogging was one of the breakout topics. As luck would have it, we were all given the assignment to write a short blog-style piece and share it with the person sitting next to us. My partner was David, a minister who blogged on the subject of fallen angels.

"Promise me you'll start blogging," David said when the session ended. "It's a supportive community, and there is nothing to be afraid of."

I promised. And then I did begin blogging, mostly because I did not want to lie to a man of the cloth. My website, www.elderskelter.net, was designed with help from my very talented friend Sarah. I knew that an important lifeline had been thrown my way.

My first post appeared on April 1, 2015. It was titled "Roll It Up and Run!" and told the story of the rainy day and Greg's poster project. I began to blog on an almost weekly basis, about how caring for my mom was affecting me and my family. I tossed in some nostalgia and humor in an effort to keep it upbeat. To my relief, the comments I received were encouraging. I had not expected such a strong outpouring of support.

A few weeks after beginning my blog, I attended an evening event at the local grammar school. I needed to write a small feature story on it as part of my at-home consulting job for the local grammar schools.

I am a big baby about evening events. They involve putting on pants with actual zippers and checking that there is no food in my teeth.

I arrived and sat down near a neighborhood acquaintance named Dawn Marie who immediately mentioned my blog.

"My parents passed years ago, but I really do enjoy reading about you and your mom," she said. "Every time I read your blog, I get something out of it."

I expressed my gratitude and was relieved. When I began blogging, I reminded myself that some of the close friends who commented on my blog posts and read them loyally had lost either one or both of their parents at an early age. Partly in deference to them, I tried to keep the "woe is me" aspect to a minimum. I was silently congratulating myself when Dawn Marie said something else.

"I love that you're keeping it light, but you have to make it more real."

I was stunned. Dawn Marie was sharp and honest. I knew in my heart that she was one hundred percent correct. My blog kept it light, but my life at that moment was anything but. I cried often, trying to figure out what was going wrong. Caring for my mom was taking a lot more out of me than I had anticipated, and I just wasn't sure why.

I was about to reply when the ceremony started. I realized that community volunteers were being honored along with student scholars and athletes. And one of the volunteers was the husband of another neighborhood acquaintance named Carol.

Carol had twins the same age as Greg, and we'd crossed paths many a time. I knew Carol to be the kind of person you could trust with your life. "Warm" and "kind" are the adjectives people most often used to describe her. Carol's husband was there to receive an award for his years of service in the town's first-aid squad.

Carol approached me after the ceremony. She had read my blog and had some news to tell me.

She was making a career change and entering the field of in-home elder care.

You know those movies where the skies open up and light from the heavens comes flooding in? All that was missing was Moses holding a staff and parting the seas.

I asked Carol if she would consider caring for my mom on an as-needed basis. Carol agreed, and within a few weeks John and I were able to spend quality time—as in a full day and evening—out and about together. Carol, with her delicious home-made foods and upbeat attitude and attentiveness, turned out to provide a mini-vacation for Mom as well. They developed a kinship.

One day Carol encouraged me to reach out to the local office on aging to see if we qualified for any services (we did). With their assistance, we received a much-needed source of support as well as access to respite care. Respite care actually represents respite for the care*givers*, while your elderly loved one takes an enforced mini-vacation at a local nursing home. What a concept!

Feeling bolstered by these new sources of support and care, I took Dawn Marie's advice. I included the word *dementia* in a blog post.

At first I flinched. And then I smiled.

The comments I received in response brought me to a higher level of communication and affirmation than I had ever known. I began opening up more in conversations with friends and relatives, instead of pretending that I was leading some sort of charmed life.

This included my friend Andrea, who phoned one day just to check in. We live far apart, and we miss one another. During this catch-up phone call, I told Andrea that Veronica would be spending the spring semester of her junior year studying abroad in Alcalá, Spain. John, coincidentally, would be traveling to Barcelona, Spain, on business at some point during that time. John wanted to make a real vacation of it by taking me with him to Barcelona. We would then visit Alcalá to spend some time with Veronica.

John and I tried to work it out. But we couldn't manage the financial or logistical part of it. Mom didn't have enough days of free respite care, and with me working only part time from home, we couldn't justify the expense. During the phone call, I told Andrea how excited we had been about the possibility of the three of us traveling together in Spain. And I told her how disappointed I was that we couldn't work it out. The old me would have never revealed the depth of my sadness. The Mandricks, my clan, had no patience for complainers. My dad was especially disdainful of them. Here I was, breaking the rules. I immediately tried to backtrack. "But it's fine, really," I added.

Andrea felt otherwise.

"If it's not fine with you, then it's *not* fine," she said. "And it's okay to say so. I wish I could change this for you. You're working so hard to take care of your mom, and you deserve a break. I totally get it, and I understand your disappointment."

And there it was. I was empowered by Andrea's affirmation that my feelings did indeed matter, and that sometimes it did have to be about me. Andrea, as much as she wanted to, couldn't make things better. But *I* could. I couldn't achieve my dream of vacationing in Spain. But I could tackle another dream, one that I'd had for a while.

Once again, God was working in mysterious ways. I'd been denied the gift of autonomy, at least for a while. But I'd been given the gift of free time. It was so obvious, I almost laughed. And then I took the first step. I began writing this book.

Chapter Eight

"I'm Tired"

THERE IS A SONG THAT MADELINE KAHN PERFORMED IN the movie *Blazing Saddles* that never fails to crack me up. The incomparable Madeline, as a character named Lili Von Shtupp and in a spoof of Marlene Dietrich, sings about being worn out by unsatisfying romantic liaisons with men.

"I'm tired, tired of playing the game, ain't it a crying shame, I'm tired."

In the film, it was salty and funny. In real life, not so much.

Here is the version of "I'm Tired" I used to sing when Mom lived with us, sans the sultry look and sexy ensemble.

I'm tired of never finishing my second cup of coffee because Mom is up and needs breakfast.

I'm tired of Mom asking where I am going every time I leave the house for a walk, grocery shopping, exercise class, coffee with a friend, or other diversion.

I'm tired of trying to balance Mom's needs for in-home comfort with John's needs for out-of-the-house socializing.

I'm tired of not being able to hop in my car and take a day trip or an overnight to see either of my children who are in different states.

I'm tired of telling acquaintances that I am not technically an empty-nester when they ask if my house is quiet with the kids gone.

I'm tired of Mom not being able to follow more than one direction at a time and having to repeat even that single direction for her.

I'm tired of Mom flinching and complaining every time a curse word is uttered during my favorite TV shows.

I'm tired of feeling like I am pulling into an office complex to report for work, when in fact I am sitting in the car in my own driveway and dreading entering the house to start Mom's care routine.

I'm tired of not traveling, when this was the long-anticipated time when John and I figured I could finally accompany him on business trips.

I'm tired of spending limited quality time both inside and outside the house.

I'm tired of waking up multiple times in the middle of the night when I hear Mom gripping the handrails we installed in the hallway so she can make it to the bathroom safely.

I'm tired of those moments—once rare but increasingly frequent—when I wonder how much longer I can do this.

Let's face it: I was pooped. As my mother-in-law Dolly used to say, "Too much is too much." She spent years caring for her mother and her stepfather when she was in her mid-forties. After that, when Dolly was in her early fifties, her widowed mother-in-law, known as Oma, became forgetful and had to move in. Oma was a force of nature, and, in her own way, Dolly was just as strong-willed.

Visiting John's parents at the time when Oma was in residence was like watching a bullfight and never being sure which one was the bull. Oma was strong-willed and sort of sneaky, and Dolly was miserable during the Oma years. Sadly, Dolly passed away at the age of sixty-two. After caring for one set of parents after another and then returning to work in an office, Dolly only got to enjoy about five of her golden years. She did her time, so to speak, and never really got to reap the rewards. I thought about Dolly only about a million times when Mom was living with me. The thought of stepping off the elder care treadmill and into the gates of heaven scared the stuffing out of me.

But here is the other side of the coin. I finally learned to make the most of every minute I have been given and to worry much less about what the future has in store.

With Mom under my roof, I began watching movies all the way through and getting lost in them. I earned the satisfaction of preparing home-cooked meals more often rather than paying a small fortune for weekday takeout dinners. I learned the art of cocooning—shutting out the rest of the world. I played along to *Wheel of Fortune* and *Jeopardy!* shouting out the answers for Mom's entertainment. I learned to make the most of my limited time for social events and outings. I enjoyed them more and didn't worry so much about how I looked and acted. I tackled the crocheting and sewing and writing projects I had thought about for years. And, thanks to my mother's enduring love and appreciation, now so simple and pure because of her dementia, I began valuing myself more as a person in my own right and not as a conduit to someone else's happiness. Mom's brain was finally set on "relax," if not one hundred percent of the time, then at least eighty percent. Mom could still be judge-y. But it was less frequent, and not as much of it was directed at me or my family. (But let's all take a moment to pity the female news anchors, who always seem to wearing the wrong shade of lipstick, according to Mom.)

Be productive. Be helpful. Be nice. Be proactive. Be better-informed. Be spontaneous. Be a planner. Be creative. Be supportive. Be reliable. Be sociable. Be useful. Be the life of the party.

So says my inner voice.

"Shut up!" I am finally yelling back.

Mom's twenty-four-seven presence in my life for four years, and my need to focus almost totally on her care, helped me discover the truth.

Sometimes, all I really needed was to be.

While living with me, Mom often said that she missed my in-laws, Dolly and Otto. She said she missed my sister-in-law Robin's parents, Carole and Bill. She said she missed her always-funny brother Mike and her beautiful sisters-in-law Bernice and Gladys. She expressed regret about not being able to make the long trip to visit my dad's only surviving sister, the always-kind Betty. She would often gaze at the photo of my dad on the buffet in my dining room and blow a kiss as she passed it.

Mom never said she missed her nephew Michael or her niece Barbara's husband Chris. It's not that she didn't love them. She adored them, naturally, and she would have been devastated by their deaths if she could actually have grasped what happened. I did try to tell her a few times, but then I put it aside. Why upset someone when you know they won't remember it the next day? The bottom line was, anyone who passed after the year 2013 simply didn't show up on her now-impaired radar, and there was nothing I could do about it. Nor, in fact, should I.

It took me a while to realize that in addition to taking away some of her edge, dementia also robbed my mother of the ability to mourn. And for that, I don't know whether to kiss dementia or slap it.

Chapter Nine

From Soup to Nuts

IN THE FALL OF 2008, I WAS IN THE THICK OF THINGS AS far as "sandwiching"—caring for two generations at once—was concerned. My son was in his first year of high school, and my daughter had just begun eighth grade. My parents were still living in their apartment in Long Branch, but they were no longer able to make the twenty-minute walk to the food store or the doctor's office. I was working part-time as an assistant librarian at the local grammar school, with afternoons off.

"Off" might be the incorrect word here. On afternoons, I began my second job as personal assistant to my aging parents. To be fair, it was only two afternoons a week. Yet the emotion attached to navigating this unfamiliar territory drained me mentally and physically.

On one such afternoon, I entered the foyer of my parents' apartment and knocked on the door, praying Mom would hear and answer quickly. I worried that my father—nearly blind from macular degeneration and unsteady on his feet due to his advanced age—would hear the knock and attempt to answer the door before Mom could stop him.

"I'll bet she's in the bathroom again," I said to myself. Either I had the most unfortunate timing—often arriving and knocking on their door just as Mom was in the bathroom—or Mom spent a lot of time in there. I was betting on the latter. Mom was a big one for primping and for last-minute touch-ups before heading out anywhere. "Can I choke down a cup of cawfee?" was her usual refrain when I was a teenager and impatient to get out of the house with her for a shopping spree at Sears or an appointment with my dermatologist or some other earth-shattering event.

To my relief, Mom answered and let me in. I noticed her freshly applied lipstick and did an eye roll in my mind before heading to say hello to Dad and get him moving along. We were scheduled for an appointment with my dad's heart doctor and a blood check, with a "quick" trip to the food store afterward. I had finished up my part-time job at the local school library and was at their service until dinnertime.

"Are you feeling okay?" my dad asked.

I sighed. I had headed home quickly after work to change into my stretchy sweatpants. I did not relish the thought of showing up at a doctor's office and being on display at the local Foodtown dressed the way I was. But the maneuvering required to get both of my parents out of the apartment and onto our rounds involved a lot of bending and stretching on my part. My somewhat sedentary job had resulted in weight gain around my waistline. I reasoned that I simply could not deal with an endless wait at the doctor's office and following mom around the Foodtown in endless circles while dealing with too-tight slacks.

My father felt otherwise. "Are you feeling okay?" was code that I was familiar with. It meant that I was not looking my best. My father wore belted slacks, nice shoes, a clean collared shirt, and a vest or sweater every day and had for years. His own father had sported a suit and fedora on most occasions, except when he was working as the engineer of a coal train. Dad and Grandpa would have to be feeling pretty darn lousy, flu-like at the least, to let their standards slip in any way. Dad's high standards showed in his mode of dress, his always graceful and soft-spoken manner, and his ability to keep unpleasant thoughts to himself in almost any situation. Mom dressed impeccably as well. In all of my years, from childhood until my mom moved in with us, I had never seen her or my dad in pajamas or underwear. It was as though they went to sleep in glass pods wearing their street clothes and woke up with them steamed and pressed.

Even when caring for my dad left her totally wrung out, my mother made sure they were both dressed and washed immediately upon awakening. And she kept their Long Branch apartment just as clean as her home had been.

My mother's fixation on sparkling clean once compelled me to call out sick in high school, pretending to be her on the phone to the school secretary, so I could watch television all day while I paste waxed her living room and bedroom furniture and cleaned her oven. At the time she was working long hours at the factory and had expressed concern about her inability to take care of these matters. One of our unofficial family mottos was, "We're sometimes broke, but always clean."

With my father's arm through mine for support and my mother bringing up the rear, we all walked carefully along the hundred-foot path to the parking lot. I bundled my sharply dressed parents into the car and headed to the doctor's office a few blocks away. My dad had a pacemaker and was taking a blood thinner, which resulted in the need for regular checks of his blood levels. He once landed in the hospital on Christmas Day due to a detected imbalance.

"Mr. Mandrick?" the nurse called out in the crowded waiting room, and I helped Dad shuffle in for his blood test. It was the finger prick. I had endured enough of those in my grade school years when my blood's B12 levels mysteriously plummeted.

I silently thanked God that I now checked out fine and did not have to endure the nasty experience my dad was having. I looked away instinctively, and I knew he was finished when he thanked the nurse.

That's what he did. He told every nurse in that office who pricked his finger that she had done a terrific job, and offered a sincere thank you. Every single time.

Once my parents were deposited back in the car, it was time for the second round. The Foodtown was just a few blocks from the doctor's office, and Dad was content to sit in the car with the windows slightly open—sort of like a dog, really—while Mom and I did a "quick" food shop.

"Have fun," he said cheerfully, happy for the peace and an opportunity for some shut-eye.

I smiled at Dad and looked back as Mom and I crossed the lot. I wished his contentment were contagious.

I took a deep breath to prepare for the task at hand. The air was warm but not overly so, and a refreshing breeze was coming in off the ocean. Even though we were a few blocks from the beach, I could smell the salty air, and it had a relaxing effect. I convinced myself that I was ready for action. I began to steer Mom, by the elbow, toward the row of carts outside the Foodtown, which never failed to amaze me with its array of clientele: beautiful dark-haired women of Syrian Jewish descent, most of them young mothers with carts full of adorable and very obedient children; frail-looking elderly men and women making their way slowly through the aisles with the help of all manner of walking aids (including the elbows of their middle-aged children); giddy college students from nearby Monmouth University buying a combination of healthy veggies, salty snack foods, and lots of frozen meals; aging surfer dudes with long gray ponytails packing whatever they could cram into the store's signature blue tote baskets (they were too cool for carts, apparently); and fast-moving hospital workers and day laborers trying to fit in a quick bout of food shopping between shifts.

Into this melting pot of characters looking to get around or away from one another entered the dynamic duo of Mom and Mary Ann. Mom proceeded to walk her shopping cart not even five feet down the narrow aisle from the entrance door and come to an abrupt halt, trying to get her bearings in a store she had visited at least one hundred times. Two other shoppers attempted to avoid careening into her and ended up toppling into one another instead. I looked at Mom's latest victims warily and apologetically and saw anger in their eyes.

"Keep going, you can't stop short," I said to Mom, both miffed and embarrassed. Must we go through this routine every single time? I thought, even though I knew the answer.

Mom's clueless yet determined expression said it all. Now I understood why, when Mom shopped at our local Valley Fair store back in the day, my dad headed to the conveniently located bar near the sprawling department store's music section where I sorted through the forty-five RPM vinyl. Neither of us wanted to witness the painful spectacle of my somewhat befuddled mother tossing items into her cart, only to stop a few minutes later to say, "Now, who put *that* in there? I wanted sugar-free gelatin!" As if there were some invisible person determined to screw up my mother's shopping trip and our food enjoyment. I have always suspected my mother had some form of attention deficit disorder, and let's just say it really bit her in the butt during food forays. I eventually ended up working in a food store and pretty much failed as a cashier. I was removed from cash register duty and relegated to doing returns. This exciting duty involved taking unpurchased items from grocery carts and returning them to the shelves. The next time you change your mind about purchasing that can of baked beans after you have reached the register, you have someone like me to thank for putting them back. You're welcome. Thanks to my failure as a cashier and my mother's years of totally irritating me in food stores, I despise the process of grocery shopping.

I grabbed my mother's elbow to move her along. Once she was on her way and unleashed on what would surely be more hapless victims, I mumbled something about needing groceries myself. I hightailed it to the other end of the store, and with good reason. My mother always shopped without a list; this resulted in the examination of pretty much every item in the store and a decision on whether it was cart-worthy. If she left an aisle and then remembered that she actually did need something stocked there, she would head back for it no matter where else she was in the store. The overall effect is that on every single shopping trip, my mom ended up zigging and zagging across the entire length of the store, similar to a duck in a shooting gallery.

A few times I tried to help by suggesting she make a list, and she shooed me away like I was a pesky fly.

Forty minutes into this shopping trip, I was killing time in the health and beauty aisle by reading the label of a shampoo bottle when my cell phone rang. I did not recognize the number, but I answered anyway.

It was Greg, using someone else's cell phone. He proceeded to tell me he had forgotten to charge his own cell phone. Oh, and soccer practice ended early and he needed a ride home. And the friend whose cell phone he was using needed a ride home as well.

"Well, I am out shopping with Grammy," I explained. "I can rush her along but I won't be there for at least another half hour."

Greg sighed, and so did I.

Locating my mother was somewhat easily accomplished; I just had to do a quick jog past ten aisles and search for the plump and very pretty lady who looked like a grandmother straight out of Central Casting. I found her in the soup aisle and walked up behind her, dreading the unpleasant task of telling the world's most adorable little old lady that she needed to wrap it up. Over forty minutes would be enough time for most folks to complete a food run, but not for mom. Add in the effects of aging, and she was practically shopping in reverse.

Mom was in the process of examining cans of chicken noodle soup on the shelf when I told her about my dilemma. She sighed but reported that chicken soup was the last item she needed. I silently thanked God and tried to help move things along. I rummaged through until I found a few suitable cans of chicken noodle soup.

She frowned when she saw them. "Not those," she said. "Daddy likes the skinny noodles."

"Does it say skinny noodles on the label?" I asked, trying to make a joke but also getting frustrated.

"Yes, it says skinny noodles," she said.

"No, it doesn't," I argued. "I have never seen a can of soup that says skinny noodles on it." I said this as though I had spent my life buying soup. Truthfully, I do not eat it and therefore have rarely picked a can up off the shelf.

The after-four rush had begun, and more shoppers were steering their carts down the soup aisle. I remembered my friend Peter making fun of the elderly people always hunched down in front of the soup cans, blocking the aisle and aggravating the other shoppers. That was back when my dad could drive and take my mother food shopping. I would laugh with Peter, but secretly I suspected my mother was one of these annoying people.

As I hunched down and scrutinized more soup labels, my butt sticking out unattractively and my hair making a frizzy halo about my head, I had a sudden chilling realization—now *I* was one of those old people hunched in front of the soup. I was probably aggravating the other customers. Perhaps they were silently mocking me. This horrid thought sent me reaching blindly and desperately for another can of chicken noodle soup. It was "homestyle," whatever that meant. I was hoping it meant skinny noodles.

I handed it to my mother roughly, as if this had better be the end of it. She looked at me as though I had lost my mind.

"This isn't it," she said, and she placed the can right back on the shelf. Then, effortlessly, gracefully, she extracted three cans from the group next to the now-rejected can. "See?" she said, holding them up triumphantly before thrusting them into her cart. To my utter shock, the label said, "Chicken soup with skinny noodles."

I turned around to see if I was being pranked. No such luck. I was just living another day as a Baby Boomer caught between caring for growing children and for elderly parents. And not doing a spectacularly amazing job at either.

At the checkout, the cashier regarded us with a somewhat mournful expression. Was she feeling my pain? "Oh, is this your daughter?" she asked my mom.

"Yes, she is very good to me," my mother said proudly while I threw her items onto the conveyor belt. I noticed that my mother had not even reached into her purse to pull out her wallet. Unlike me, she had all the time in the world.

"My mom passed away five years ago, and I wish she were still around," the cashier said sadly. She pouted, and I wanted to slap her. I also wanted to ask her if she wanted to borrow my mom for a while, or at least pack up her groceries and drive her home so I could pick up my son who was now standing on a hot soccer field and cursing his luck at having me for a mother. But I did not. I smiled sweetly and muttered something about how fortunate I was.

Because I was. Right? And then, distracted by the fact that I thought the cashier was actually going to start crying, I accidentally dropped my ten-ton purse on top of the egg carton nestled in the seat of the cart. I heard a crunching noise and was paralyzed with embarrassment.

My eighty-year-old mother lifted my purse off the broken egg carton. She frowned and said, "Why is this thing always so heavy?"

I thought about making that offer I was thinking about to the cashier, with a no-return policy. The cashier examined the eggs inside the carton, at least half of them now ruined, and ordered me to retrieve another carton of eggs from the dairy aisle.

"Any lady as sweet and pulled-together as your mom deserves beautiful unbroken eggs," the cashier said.

I gritted my teeth and continued trotting over to the dairy aisle while almost knocking over an elderly man. So much for grace under pressure. He glared at me as I apologized. I apologized again, but he was still scowling. So I continued on my way, sweating slightly and making a silent tally of everyone I had failed that day thus far. Greg, who was waiting patiently for a ride while I was busy breaking eggs. Dad, sitting in the car for almost an hour because I had let Mom shop on her own. Mom, whose eggs I had broken and who I, frankly, didn't feel bad for. And that made me feel worse. And the cashier, because deep down I suspected that she liked her mother a lot more now that she was gone. Shame on me, I thought, for all of it. I reached for the new carton of eggs, red-faced. I had to take a deep breath to keep from crying.

An incident a week later brought home the fact that I was not alone in my supermarket suffering.

It was an unusually hot day for mid-September, and the air-conditioning unit in the Foodtown was, like the rest of us, feeling the strain. Sweat poured off my brow as I made my way through the aisles, hoping to move faster but feeling like my feet were mired in something sticky. Had someone spilled honey? It sure felt like it. It seemed every shopper was suffering as much as I was. Every one of them appeared shiny-faced and miserable, except one older woman who caught my eye as I made my way down the cereal aisle toward the courtesy counter. Her silver hair was piled artfully atop her head, extending her already impressive height. Perfectly applied makeup accentuated her chiseled features and pale blue eyes. While her sequin-embellished pale blue track suit outfit seemed a bit much for the hot weather, she appeared as cool as a cucumber. She was chatting animatedly, waving her arms at the representative standing behind the courtesy counter. The older lady was saying something about a courtesy card. Before the representative could reply, I saw another woman walking toward them. Her blonde layered hair was unruly and damp where it reached her shoulders, her face was beet red, and she kept glancing back at a packed shopping cart lined up for a checkout.

"Mom," the woman called as she made her way over, and I could see she was sweating mightily despite the fact that she was wearing a tank top and shorts. "I told you, Mom, you can use *my* courtesy card to get the savings today."

The older lady waved her hand dismissively. "I need my *own* card," she said, and I recognized the tone. Defiant, instructive, and just a tad belittling. Well, maybe more than a tad.

The woman's daughter looked toward the cart, and then the door to the outside. "Dad is in the car in the parking lot, Mom, and it's sweltering. We need to get going now!"

"Well!" the older woman huffed. "Turn on the air conditioning for him." *Idiot*, she may as well have added. She turned toward the courtesy counter, determined to hold that dang courtesy card in her hand, despite everyone else's discomfort. Her daughter, realizing defeat with a wild-eyed last look at the courtesy counter, ran outside. I am sure she doubted that she would find her father still breathing.

I had a pit in my stomach and turned my cart away from the scene at the courtesy counter. I knew the situation had nothing to do with me personally, yet every fiber of my being felt the hurt and betrayal that was so evident in the frantic woman's eyes. I wondered why the scene affected me so strongly, and then I realized something. I could almost see my mom doing that. It was as though caring for my aging dad had turned her into someone else, someone more assertive and demanding. Maybe at a certain point in life, strong-willed women who had submitted to others' needs for years finally had enough and decided to put themselves first. If so, the older woman's daughter and I were collateral damage. It didn't seem fair, and I felt angry. I pushed my cart forward and continued my shopping.

I wasn't pleased to see that the older lady was preparing to pay for her groceries just ahead of me in the checkout line. I noticed the way she performed every task with a flourish, as though she were onstage. *If this is what other daughters have to deal with on a regular basis, I have a lot to be thankful for.* I had spent at least ten minutes food shopping after witnessing the shakedown at the courtesy counter, which meant that was how long her daughter had been sitting in the car trying to keep her dad alive. I sighed and said a silent prayer for a woman I didn't know. When the older lady finally paid for her order, she walked away breezily. The aroma of expensive scented powder and victory flavored the air.

"Lord help us," I said out loud, without meaning to.

"What did you say?" the cashier asked, confused.

I thought about some of my traits that rankled Mom. *You're too sensitive. You feel sorry for the wrong people. You worry about things you shouldn't. You get too involved in other people's troubles. You need to stop trying to save the world and tackle the problems in your own backyard.*

I looked at the cashier, who was eyeing me warily. I suddenly felt very small.

"Nothing," I answered. "Nothing at all."

Chapter Ten

The Lure of the Urologist

I FEEL LIKE I SHOULD HAVE SEEN SIGNS OF MY MOTHER'S impending dementia way before I did. One episode that comes to mind occurred in 2009.

For eleven years, from September 2002 until my dad's passing in April 2013, my parents lived in an apartment on the ocean in nearby Long Branch. I phoned them to check in at nine p.m. every night, which could be stressful. Mom had a habit of inserting disturbing news or a perplexing question near the end of every phone conversation.

One of our conversations, on an evening in the winter of 2009, went something like this:

"Hi, Mom. How are you?"

"Well, I just received a card in the mail today. The lurologist moved. I don't know where the new office is."

Someone less savvy to my mom's unique communication skills may have heard this statement and believed that my nearly blind, ninety-one-year-old dad had taken up fishing. Not only that, but he hired someone to make him special lures. Of course, I knew better. This was a case of my mother handing me a trifecta.

1. An unpleasant surprise.

2. A malapropism.

3. Too little information, and most likely delivered too late as well.

Up until that point, I had no idea my father was seeing the urologist. It turned out that my mother had gamely been taking him in a taxicab to appointments in the same building where their primary doctor was located, for God only knew how long. All of this was established in this late-evening conversation, along with my mother's solemn vow that she had no idea why Daddy needed to see a lurologist. But apparently it had something to do with his "numbers."

It was hard work to convince my mother that the doctor's new office was too far away for them to take a cab, which was not a good idea anyway, since they both now had issues with walking and with balance. I called the doctor's office and made an appointment.

A few days later we arrived for a consultation, and the doctor in his blue scrubs and colorful Crocs was running on schedule. The four of us sat in an examining room as he detailed my father's history. He provided me with a brief summary of office visits dating back at least five years and glanced at me as he mentioned my father's numbers.

I must have appeared perplexed, because he said, "You are aware that your father has prostate cancer, aren't you?"

I could not utter a sound. The news hit me like a ton of bricks. I had recently lost a dear friend to that disease. Although I know it is one of the most treatable cancers, I was frightened beyond belief. Slack-jawed, I glanced at my dad and then at my mom—who gazed wide-eyed at the doctor and said, "He has *what?*"

The doctor looked like he wanted to fling his happy Crocs right at my mother's head. Instead he took a moment to compose himself. My hard-of-hearing dad was sitting on the examining table, following this all with his usual expression of nonchalance. I was not sure if he heard what the doctor said, but I hoped he hadn't. The doctor stared back at my mom.

"You did tell your daughter that your husband has prostate cancer," he said as if assuring himself that this statement just had to be true.

She turned to me. "He has *what*?" she said. "I don't understand."

So many thoughts were going through my head. My father had cancer. Why hadn't my mother told me? Did she not understand? Was she trying to protect me? Was she in shock? I am embarrassed to admit that the thought she could be suffering from some brain-related distress such as Alzheimer's or dementia never crossed my mind. After all, she was caring for my dad with minimal help from me, setting out his medication and preparing meals and keeping track of doctor's appointments. Knowing my mom's reputation for stealth behavior, I settled on *She was protecting me*. It was the most logical choice and the easiest to accept—especially since I was still struggling with the diagnosis.

My utter confusion must have made me appear out of it, because now the doctor's eyes settled on my dad. Dad always managed to appear composed in all situations, and I am sure the doctor was wondering how the almost-blind elderly man, who moments ago had to be helped onto the examining table, was the sharpest knife in our family drawer.

I saw my dad's peaceful face, and somehow the fog of fear lifted and I was able to formulate some thoughts.

My eighty-two-year-old mother had been scheduling cab rides and taking my dad on visits to the urologist on her own, without involving me. I had to give her credit for that. In another stroke of luck, the urologist had moved to a different office at the right time. I was brought into the situation exactly when my help was needed. I was actually grateful for the timing and my mother's perseverance. I was also grateful that my father had progressed to a ripe old age before getting seriously bad news from any doctor. I was grateful that my mom and myself were in good health and would be able to do whatever it took to help him fight the disease. I focused my attention on the doctor and asked, "Where do we go from here?"

Relieved, the doctor gave us our action plan. I needed to get my dad to the local hospital for a test that would tell us if the cancer had spread to his bones. We had to schedule regular appointments for injections of hormones that would help to curb the spread of the cancer. And above all, we needed to follow through and stop acting as though he did not have cancer. (That last statement may have been directed at my mother.)

I was in a daze as we exited the office. It had started to rain, as if on cue, and I felt like the dark sky I could see from the waiting room windows reflected my frame of mind. So much to take in, so much to do, and how would he respond to treatment? All the while, my mother kept asking me what the doctor had said, as if she hadn't been in the room with us. Suddenly my cell phone pinged with an arriving text message.

I deposited my parents in chairs in order to bring the car around to the front of the building and checked the text to make sure it had not come from one of my teenage children. It was a photo sent from my wonderful sister-in-law Robin of an exquisite emerald-colored vase adorned with gold and with yellow and red flowers. It was breathtaking. It glowed like a beacon from the heavens sent to lift my spirits on that gloomy day. Aware of my love of all things green and glass, she had bought it for me.

Do you like it? she asked in the text. I almost cried. It was breathtaking. Although Robin was unaware of the events that had recently unfolded and therefore had not sent the photo in response to my distress, it certainly served as a sign that someone up there was watching out for the three of us.

I sent a text assuring her that I loved it and was so grateful. Of course, her message was a reminder that I would soon have the task of telling my husband, our kids, and our close family and friends—all of whom adored my father, and most of whom had lost loved ones far too early to cancer—that he had been diagnosed. But I reminded myself to live in the moment. So I smiled at the photo and message, retrieved the car, and bundled my parents inside.

Following our tradition of having a treat after every doctor's office visit, my parents and I immediately headed to the nearest doughnut shop, where my mother dominated the conversation. Dad still managed to toss out more than his share of ancient one-liners. Mom and I managed to laugh at each one of them, but it took some effort.

And then Mom announced that Dad needed handkerchiefs. I hate the thought of handkerchief usage, and I hate buying them as well. They are unhygienic and hard to locate. I was tempted to sigh. But not this time. I was exhausted but also in need of some kind of diversion.

"Dad needs handkerchiefs? Road trip!" I announced.

A half hour later, with Dad snoozing happily in the car, my mother and I set off on the strangely reassuring and life-affirming task of buying Dad his bleeping handkerchiefs.

"This is going to be a lot for you," she said, to my surprise.

Wait, Mom did know about the cancer? Like the gambler I am, I knew better than to show my hand.

"What do you mean?" I asked, proud of my caginess, if that is indeed a word.

"You know, driving dad every few weeks to get those shots and all." She shrugged.

I wasn't sure if she wasn't getting it or if she was just protecting me. Out of fear or laziness or most likely both, I never tried to get at the truth of the matter.

Throughout his course of treatment, which lasted from 2009 through his death in April 2013, the word *cancer* was never mentioned by Mom or Dad. It did, however, appear on Dad's death certificate. My mother insisted on caring for Dad herself, in their apartment, and she did so until the day he died. Although I knew that it was what Mom wanted, I realize in retrospect that it was way too much for her to take on. I should have realized it that day. Perhaps I was in denial. In any case, I still feel enormous guilt about leaving them alone in the apartment on that day and those that followed. I should have stepped up and insisted they move in with my family, or hired nursing care. It's an uncomfortable feeling that I don't believe I'll ever shake.

After the shopping trip, I phoned John to say that the day had gotten away from us, and I would be picking up takeout to eat with my parents. I said nothing about Dad's diagnosis, as I wanted to tell John in person. After I left my parents that evening, I did something I often felt compelled to do when the weather permitted. I walked down the path leading from their apartment facing the ocean to the boardwalk nearby. I looked back and saw the lights blazing in their cozy apartment. There was something about my parents that people found reassuring. It was as though they made the light shine brighter, and you wanted to join them and bask in it.

"You are very lucky," a stranger had told the three of us just weeks before as we dined at the buffet in Atlantic City during a day's getaway. At first I thought she was addressing my parents. But then she gave me a wistful look.

Wistful was what I felt at that moment, staring at the lights from my vantage point on the deserted boardwalk. Although I knew it was not possible, part of me hoped that both of my parents could forever be found in that space. In that peaceful place, my dad would be endlessly watching TV, and my mother would be sitting on the sofa nearby, crocheting yet another blanket to give to me or one of my children, or maybe even to my very spoiled cat.

For years I believed I was a strong person, cheerful and optimistic no matter what was occurring in my life. Sometimes I attributed this to the fact that I do really try to help others as much as I can, and I was somehow being rewarded. Other times I believed what my mother is still fond of telling me: that the grandmother I never met, my father's mother Jeannette, was a very cheerful person at all times, and I was just like her. I chose to believe this, naturally, since it seemed like such a lucky thing. Yes, I thought I had been handed the prized Cheerfulness Gene.

Now I knew the truth. I'd lived a very charmed life, and for a very long time. It was not perseverance or strength of character that had put an almost-constant smile on my face.

It was sheer luck.

Chapter Eleven

It's Good to Be the King!

IN 2009, WE LEARNED THAT DAD'S PACEMAKER NEEDED replacing. I was worried, but as usual Dad came through like a trooper at the age of ninety-one. The nurses fawned over him as they guided his wheelchair toward us in the waiting room from the recovery area, marveling at his good color and his bright blue eyes and his obvious good health. I knew once we reached the car he would spring out of that thing like a coiled viper in order to prove that no wheelchair was necessary for Joe Mandrick. Lucky Joe Mandrick relied on his cane and what John called the "human chain" of John, Mom, and me.

"Look at him, like a king on his throne," John said as Dad and his entourage sailed down the hall. And for the first time ever, I sensed a note of jealousy along with the usual admiration in John's voice. I had to laugh, because John wasn't the first person to feel that way. My mom silently fumed during many a Mandrick family gathering as his three sisters fawned over him. "Oh, *Joey!*" they would exclaim at the end of one of his jokes, their eyes shining. Dad wouldn't allow Mom to call him "Joey." He didn't care for that nickname. But my aunts were given free reign. Dad would cut out his tongue before saying anything to hurt his sisters' feelings. They were a loyal clan, those Mandricks. They clung to one another like barnacles, and I suspect it's because they had to.

One of Dad's earliest memories was sitting in the sidecar of a motorcycle with his father as they headed from Hoboken, New Jersey, into Lyndhurst, New Jersey.

My grandpa Joe's best friend was the owner of the motorcycle, and he was doing the Mandrick family a favor. He was delivering my grandpa Joe and my dad to their newest rental, this time in Lyndhurst. Grandpa Joe hated to paint walls. As in, despised. And so the Mandricks were forced to move to another rental residence whenever the walls needed a freshening. I kid you not. I have no idea where my grandmother Jeannette was on this occasion, but I assume she was trying to unpack boxes and deal with her three young daughters while making the best of a crazy situation. For all I know, she may have been reveling in it. The Mandricks were eccentrics of the highest order. But sometimes, what sounds funny actually isn't.

My father never complained about his parents or referred to them as eccentric. But he once confessed that all of this moving about was, for him, extremely unsettling. He fell in love with that rented house and the town of Lyndhurst, only to have to leave a few years later when the walls needed painting. Almost every time we visited cities and towns in Hudson County, from the time I was a child through when I was a grown woman, Dad would point out places where he had once lived or schools he had attended. The one I remember most clearly was a large brick building in Weehawken, New Jersey, with large windows and oodles of charm combined with gritty appeal. Dad identified it as his former school, and the signage told us it had been converted to condominiums available for sale. Usually when Dad identified a former home or school, he attempted to sound chipper about it. He made light of the fact that his dad was seldom around and that most of his childhood memories involved his mom and her large family. But on that scenic street along the palisades in Weehawken, Dad allowed disappointment and sadness to seep into his voice.

After leaving Lyndhurst when my dad was seven years old, the non-painting Mandricks ended up living in at least six more rentals before finally settling "for good" into a top-floor rental at Two Hundred South Street in the desirable Heights section of Jersey City. It was their final destination, since the landlord took it upon himself to paint the walls.

While living at Two Hundred South Street, my aunts Gladys, Bernice, and Betty sailed through high school (Dickinson) and blossomed like hothouse flowers. My father, the eldest, quit high school during his junior year and worked as a bike messenger and then at various odd jobs (including setting up the pins at a bowling alley) until he was drafted into the army. My dad returned home after serving on the front lines and performing heroic deeds that his family only learned about years later. When I was in my late twenties, my aunt Betty recalled for me the anti-climactic nature of his homecoming.

"He called from a phone booth and simply said 'I'm coming home,'" she recalled. "When our mother asked him when, he said, 'In five or ten minutes. I'm just around the corner.'"

Dad shot down any plans for a celebration, saying that the true heroes were in the ground. He received his medals in the mail and promptly hid them in a drawer where they would stay for many years. He learned that the sweetheart he had left behind had moved on. And then, after a few weeks, my dad walked from South Street in Jersey City into nearby Hoboken to try to find work.

That's where his life changed forever, making mine possible.

Chapter Twelve

Heartaches

MOM COMPLAINED FOR YEARS ABOUT HER WEDDING, COM-
paring it to her sister Millie's. "She planned everything perfectly
and even had a mirror ball at her reception," Mom would say
enviously. Dad would puff on his ever-present pipe or sip his
ever-present cup of tea or beer (Pilsner glass or mug, never from
the can) and always respond in the same way.

"Our wedding was terrific fun," he would say.

"Oh, sure, because all of *your* friends who weren't even invited
showed up and took the whole place over," Mom would say.
"The band was terrible. And our honeymoon—we went to Penn-
sylvania and all we saw was barns and cows."

"They were beautiful cows," Dad countered calmly.

"If you've seen one cow, you've seen them all," Mom shot back.

I had to laugh. I'd seen the honeymoon photos, with my
mom dressed to the nines in her usual fashion—perfectly tai-
lored dresses and suede kitten-heel shoes with ankle straps—
and Dad all duded up like a gentleman farmer. I didn't feel too
sorry for Mom. She'd lost the wedding battle, but I could see
that she'd won the war. In those photos, Dad was grinning from
ear to ear and Mom was positively glowing. Apparently they'd
done something right. And that was the key, really. They had
their differences, for sure. But for their entire lives, my parents
were entirely devoted to each other and very deeply in love.

"What wedding song did you dance to?" I asked one time when this conversation again reared its ugly head.

"'Heartaches,'" my mom answered. "Your dad's choice, he liked the rhythm."

You have to be kidding, I wanted to say. But something stopped me from laughing.

And that's because I suspected there was more to the song choice than that. My dad had endured heartaches during the war, and after. With no job and no girl, he looked for work in nearby Hoboken. As luck would have it, he met up with a friend named Harry at a local watering hole. "I heard they're hiring at the Hostess cake factory," Harry said.

Within a week, Dad was sporting a spotless white uniform and lifting endless trays off an assembly line at the Hostess factory. A somewhat gritty town with beautiful brownstones and an expansive waterfront and view of the New York City skyline, Hoboken was the setting for my parent's romance. After working at Hostess cake for a few months, Dad gazed out of a window in the large and clean factory and spotted a group of his fellow employees at a candy store across the street. They were all attractive, I am sure, in their crisp uniforms, but my mother, also a recent hire, must have been a standout with her dark auburn hair and beautiful smile. I am not exaggerating when I say that my mom has the sort of flawless face that makes everyone else's appear sort of out of whack in comparison.

Dad claims he heard a voice in his head say, "That's the girl you are going to marry," when he espied Mom. The infatuation on his end was immediate, but Mom was not an easy target.

Mom thought Dad was very handsome, but she knew he had a reputation as sort of a player. Ugh. I hated typing that sentence. But there you have it.

It took a few tries for Dad to get a date with Josephine, and she soon regretted her acquiescence.

"*I* have a date with Joe Mandrick tonight," a female coworker informed my flummoxed mom on the morning of their planned date. Mom confronted my dad.

"You had better straighten this out, Joe Mandrick," she said. (I don't know if it was because their first names could both be shortened to "Jo" and "Joe," but my mother sometimes referred to my dad as "Joe Mandrick." And my mother's brothers and their wives always referred to him as "Joe Mandrick.")

Dad did as he was told, and my parents had their first date.

On Dad's end, he must have thought things went pretty well. The next day, he suggested that Mom start making him lunches and bringing them to work. "All my girlfriends do that," he said by way of explanation.

"Make your own lunch, Joe Mandrick," Mom said. "I'm not that kind of girl."

Somehow things progressed smoothly after that initial hiccup. My somewhat judge-y grandma Anna liked my easygoing dad immediately upon meeting him. She did warn him to "never do that again" when he brought her daughter home past midnight after a date. Dad promised, and also told her that he would consider converting to the Catholic faith. This from a man who was raised as a Lutheran and taught religious classes to younger students as a teenager.

My mom must have assumed early on that she had the upper hand in this relationship. Who could blame her?

Cue the Mandrick girls, please.

Oh, the things life throws our way, just when we think we have it all figured out. My mom, long accustomed to being an iron-willed Pretty Pretty Princess, met her match and more in the Mandrick girls.

Gladys, Bernice, and Betty Mandrick—in age order—were my dad's younger sisters. I never met their mother, my paternal grandmother Jeanette DeMave. I was always aware that the

Mandrick girls were especially proud of their Dutch heritage, but I never knew much about my grandma DeMave except that my own mother adored her.

When I was in my thirties, my aunt Betty clued me in. At the time, I had young children of my own and had taken a break from working, and Aunt Betty had retired from a demanding and high-profile job. We had time to connect on a real level, and it was rewarding for both of us. Aunt Betty told me fascinating stories of our family's history, her own youth, and my father's wartime service in the infantry during World War II.

The daughter of a sailor, Jeanette DeMave grew up on a houseboat in the Netherlands (then Holland). Her parents and five siblings were dirt poor (or, on a houseboat, would you call it water poor?). Jeanette walked to school every day wearing wooden shoes and, as per her mother's orders, crocheted at the same time. (Jeanette's mother was known to all of the Mandricks as "scary Oma," just so you know.) One day eight-year-old Jeanette told her teacher that she and her family would soon be leaving for America. The teacher announced this news to the class, and then began telling her students part of a story each day. Jeanette found the story fascinating, and the teacher assured her that the story would conclude on Jeanette's last day of school before leaving for America. On that final day of school, Jeanette arrived with her mother to say goodbye to the teacher and finally hear the end of the story. But her teacher had a surprise in store.

"You have a choice, Jeanette," her teacher said, waving a small American flag. "You can hear the end of the story, or you can have this American flag." Jeanette wanted to hear the end of the story, of course; and, being nobody's fool, she immediately realized that her teacher was angry that she was betraying her country by leaving for America. Jeanette was being taunted and tested, she knew, but after weeks of waiting she still wanted desperately to hear the end of the story. And so she wavered.

"Take the flag," scary Oma hissed, and Jeanette did as she was told.

Jeanette never looked back, according to my aunt Betty. She embraced her new country and became a flag waver of the highest order, as did her son and daughters. Life in the United States wasn't always easy, but the DeMave clan raised a patriotic crew and had many success stories among them. My grandma DeMave married a man named Edward (called Joe) Mandrick, and they both worked hard to support their four children.

One of my favorite stories from my aunt Betty concerned her parents' work ethic. During the Great Depression, my grandpa Joe was one of the few people in the family fortunate enough to work steadily, and he and my grandma Jeanette helped others out financially. While raising her family, my grandma worked with an overnight crew cleaning offices in the Empire State Building in New York City. She placed my aunt Gladys in charge of her younger sisters for the evening (leading to an unfortunate life-long nervous streak in my poor sweet Aunt Gladys) and asked her to keep their secret. My grandma Jeanette made her own luck, and despite her sweet nature had no tolerance for complainers. To my cousins' and my chagrin, this was passed down to the next generation. "Let me get the crying towel," was a typical Mandrick response to any sort of sniveling.

Joe Mandrick Sr.'s family history is cloudier then Jeanette's, featuring a cast of hundreds who are related but not sure how. There were so many cousins in the Mandrick clan, we addressed longtime family friends as "cousin." For all we knew, they might well be. John still laughs about the time he drove me home from dinner when we were first dating. I decided to give him a tour of my village. "This is my cousin's house, this is my cousin's house, and so is this one," he recalls me saying as we meandered through Ridgefield Park. "You have to be kidding," I remember him saying. Nope, I wasn't.

My grandpa Joe worked for the railroad, first as a fireman and then as a train engineer. His work schedule entailed long hours away from home, and while my dad and his sisters grew up admiring their dad, they all-out adored their mom. My mother recalled her first meeting with my dad's mom and sisters as bewildering and extremely stressful.

"I felt like I was among giants," she laughed. Mom and her sister Millie both stood four feet and eleven inches tall. Grandma Jeanette and her three daughters were all five feet and eight inches tall. Gladys, Bernice, and Betty were beautiful, slim, chic, well-spoken, well-educated, and exceedingly polite. Grandma Jeanette was warm and friendly and loved to laugh. These things, for some reason, set my mother on edge.

"We were sitting there drinking coffee and eating sandwiches, and I was so nervous that I swallowed a fly rather than spitting it out," Mom said.

To be fair, there were some key differences between my mom and the Mandrick girls. For starters, despite their sharp outfits, the Mandrick girls were content with the simple things in life. They had grown up in clean but cramped apartments, and never expressed a desire for anything other than basic necessities. My aunts relished simple pleasures such as a sunny day, a bird singing, or a flower blooming. They required little in the way of creature comforts and were happy with "just enough" of everything. My mother rarely spoke negatively about her sisters-in-law, except to say that they were skinny because they "ate like birds." My father, who often ignored much of my mother's criticism, took umbrage at this every time she said it. "Birds eat twice their own weight every day," he would respond in a smarmy way, winking at me. Also, unlike my mother's D'Annunzio clan, the Mandricks were not inclined to be coddlers of husbands and, later, babies.

Many times, my mother recalled for me how she was schooled at one of the first Mandrick family gatherings she attended.

"I was making up a plate for your father," she said. "And Aunt Bernice said, 'We don't do that.'" At each retelling Mom's eyes would widen and then she would lower them, as if she was confessing to a murder or the embezzlement of a small fortune. "And so," she would end, grimacing, "I didn't do it again!" I believed the story, having lived with the Mandrick family gathering rule of "Adults eat first!"

My parents were engaged within their first year of dating, and both families, despite different religions and mindsets, hit it off splendidly. At their core, they were all good people. Sadly, I never met my grandma DeMave. She passed away in 1955, just a few years before I was born. I resemble her, and my mom tells me that I have her sense of humor. "Not everybody thinks you're funny, you know," is something my mother says to me, and I have to wonder if she sometimes thought that about her own mother-in-law. She always described her, though, as a wonderful woman who knew how to have fun.

Now, about that missing mirror ball. Dad's sisters Gladys and Bernice were both married at the time my parents were engaged, and both had planned low-key and intimate weddings. (Bernice's wedding was at the local hall called the Pierce Club, with a local band called the Dinny Barry Orchestra. Remember this, because it will become very relevant in a short while.) A few years after my parents wed, Betty would celebrate her marriage with sandwiches and drinks at the family's small but comfortable apartment at Two Hundred South Street. It wasn't that my grandmother Jeanette or Dad's sisters or Dad himself forced Mom to not go all-out on reception spending. But they did sort of lead by example. Mom had to admit, begrudgingly, that overspending on a reception was no way to start married life. So there went the mirror ball and the more expensive band and the fancier wedding hall. My parents celebrated their marriage at the popular but no-frills Pierce Club, located across the street from the Mandrick family apartment.

My mother's complaints about her wedding day were pretty much endless. My father never did convert to Catholicism, so my parents had to get married in the rectory instead of the actual church. Mom's eldest brother Mike, taking the place of her long-gone father, didn't get to walk Mom down the aisle the way he did my aunt Millie months later. In a photo that always makes me sad, Uncle Mike and my mom pose together at the entrance to the rectory. Uncle Mike is smiling widely and holding Mom's hand as he prepares to escort her inside. My mother is not smiling as widely, and her eyes show disappointment. And you remember the part about the not-up-to-snuff orchestra and my dad's friends crashing the party? Perhaps because of this, my mom appears stressed in some of the photos taken at the reception. This makes me sad, because someone not familiar with the backstory might assume that she was not excited to be marrying my dad. Nothing could have been further from the truth. They were on that day, and always, madly in love.

And then there is the terrific photo of my grandma DeMave, taking it all in from the head table in the background as my parents dance together. Grandma DeMave is absolutely glowing and has an expression on her face that my dad would describe as "the cat that swallowed the canary." Pride, love, and joy are all etched on the benevolent face of my extra-tall grandma, and I know why.

Her only son, who worked so hard to protect the freedom associated with the flag she had held in her hand so many years ago, had finally found happiness.

No more heartaches for Joe Mandrick Jr. He had just married the girl of his dreams.

Mom's tales of wedding day disappointments and debauchery were entertaining, and that's a good thing, because I certainly heard them often enough. But, of course, they stayed with me, as a reminder that careful planning helps you avoid problems (Mom), or all's well that ends well (Dad and, by extension, me). Mom wanted everything to be perfect for me on my big day. But as a member of Team Dad, I was determined to stay low-key about the wedding planning, and to not get upset if everything wasn't perfect.

The one thing we did end up agreeing on, totally by accident, was the wedding date. Forgetting that my parents' anniversary was June 4th, 1943, I booked the same day for my 1983 nuptials. Mom was thrilled, and I wasn't. In part, I actually was a little spooked about the bad wedding karma that had dogged my mom. I also did not care to share anniversaries with them.

My negative attitude about the wedding date led to trouble. I was more stressed than I should have been during the wedding planning process; my mom and I had one argument after another. One day I decided I'd had enough. I stormed out of the house and stood fuming in the backyard. To my surprise, my dad left the house and approached me. He had always avoided our mother-daughter blowups, making like the gang of would-be warriors in *Monty Python and the Holy Grail* as they prepared to storm the castle and saw that they were greatly outnumbered: "Run away, run away!"

I turned at his approach and had no idea what to expect. Hopefully, one of his famous one-liner jokes and not a rebuke.

"Your mom doesn't always have her head in the right place," he said softly. "But her heart, always. Try to remember that."

He walked away, and once again I was reminded how deeply my parents loved each other and how secure that made me feel.

Heartened by my dad's words, I actually forgot what Mom and I had been arguing about. What did details matter, really, as long as you were marrying the right person?

"All the balls will fall into place," Dad once said when I was a recent college graduate stressed about my future.

At the time, I was dismayed by the simplicity of his advice. But, as I discovered, Dad was right. Of course, he knew he was right. After all, it had happened for him.

In the end, wedding karma did make its presence known. My mom's liberal use of deodorizing spray in advance of the bridesmaids' arrival at our house caused my dad's eyes to redden to the point that he threatened to not walk me down the aisle. The wedding photographer arrived at my parents' house an hour late, and only one musician from the band we booked actually played at the reception. One of John's friends arrived in a highly inebriated state and insisted on dancing energetically with many of the guests, including my elderly great-aunts. "Ooooh, he's a great dancer!" they said as he sprayed them with sweat droplets from his chin-length hair, and I prayed that no one would break a hip. Dad was wearing his rose-colored glasses, as he had on his own wedding day. "Now that was a fun wedding!" he exclaimed, as did my father-in-law Otto, at the end of the night. I was thrilled with their pronouncement and had to agree. Although, after everything that I went through on my wedding day, I have zero tolerance for brides who complain about things like the bridesmaids' flowers not perfectly matching their dresses.

A few days after we returned from our honeymoon, we had dinner at my parents' home. I was stunned to find that my father had taken the time during my honeymoon to transform my bedroom into a music room for himself. He had set up his new man cave quite nicely, thanks to some garage sale finds, including a brown faux-suede lounge chair and a turntable system for playing his precious vinyl. It is important to note that the lounger was the only chair in the room. "There's no turning back now," a voice in my head said, and I had to smile. Dad had taken a little while to warm up to John, but the music room was a sign that his acceptance was complete.

Apparently, Dad believed that all the balls had fallen into place for me. Either that, or he sure as heck hoped they had.

Chapter Thirteen

Grey Gardens

A CHANGE WAS AFOOT IN THE SUMMER OF 2011. MY NOW-teenage children were needing me less, and my parents were needing me more. I was slipping out of the sandwich and into the pot of denture cream. I had reached the age when you look at your parents and see your future. On the whole, it wasn't pretty. As a distraction, I had planned a "fun" activity for me and my parents after an early afternoon food shop. I had the bright idea that I should drag their web-style folding lawn chairs out of the apartment's tiny living room closet and place them on a nearby patch of grass facing the ocean.

Here's where the idea went awry. I thought it would be a good idea to place my parents in these chairs so they could enjoy fresh air and sunshine. What I had forgotten is that my mother detests fresh air and sunshine, unless it involves shopping or sitting in a park and watching children play. She likes her distractions. Despite the somewhat cool breeze hitting us from the nearby ocean, Mom was soon feeling hot and irritated. She began haranguing Dad about their move to Ridgefield Park, where I grew up. The town itself and our home's location were not ideal, and the perfectionist in Mom was recounting a long list of faults for Dad's benefit. As if he was even listening.

"There was no shopping to speak of, and no buses to the malls," she said. "I couldn't drive, so your poor daughter never got to the mall. You taught your sister Bernice, though. *She* drove. We lived on that dead-end street at the bottom of a hill, and I couldn't even walk to the food store. And those ladies in town, wearing pantsuits and smoking. Some of them drank, you know. Your sister Bernice told me to never join the PTA or to bake home-made anything since the local bakery was so good, and I still wonder if I should have listened. And I couldn't wear pantsuits, not with *my* shape. Ugh. I hate my legs."

Dad didn't say a word and continued to stare at the ocean as though he expected a rescue. I did my best to tune out my mom as well. But I couldn't, and the frame of the chair was digging into my back. So much for rest and relaxation. I had brought along a crochet project, a scarf I was attempting to make for a friend. But I had not even touched it, and it sat on my lap adding to my general discomfort. I was wearing one of Dad's baseball-style caps at Mom's insistence, and it smelled like the ointment he always used to slick back his wavy hair. I noticed that the lid of the cap was slightly yellowed. Why was everything deteriorating, including the three of us? At this point, I suspected I might be aging the fastest. I had caught a glimpse of myself in the apartment's living room mirror that day and noticed that a deep crease had formed between my brows. When had that happened? Mom's continued haranguing gave me a clue.

"And you always talked to that Patty next door."

"No, I didn't," Dad said, suddenly coming back to life.

Mom grimaced. I believed him, for sure. My dad was not a talker, or a flirt. But the look on his face at that moment told me that he sort of wished he had. I closed my eyes, and my uncle's voice came into my head.

"Ooooh, Patteeeeee, he'll be baaaaack."

The year was 1975, and my uncle Paul was regaling the family sitting around my parents' kitchen table. They were playing their favorite game, Racko, while eating cheese-flavored crackers and drinking their favorite beverages. Beer for Dad and Aunt Bernice, seltzer for Uncle Paul, coffee for Mom, and tea for Aunt Gladys and Uncle Fred. I had thought the warmth I felt when being around my relatives might fade as I got older. But there I stood at the age of seventeen, thrilled that I had opened my front door to find them all in the kitchen. It was as though they'd been sitting there forever.

Upon entering the kitchen, I heard what Uncle Paul was saying and I could tell that my mother was uncomfortable. I couldn't blame her. My uncle's wit was sharp, and no one wanted to be on the pointy end.

Patty was our beautiful blonde neighbor and the mother of my first friend in the neighborhood, Brian. Brian was my defender, confidante, and first real crush until life took us down very different paths. Brian's dad, Buddy, had walked out on the family a few weeks before in order to move in with his much-younger girlfriend. Mom had made the mistake of telling everyone seated at the table that Patty had told her about it. And Mom had assured Patty that Buddy would be back.

"It's okay, Patteeeee, he'll be baaaack," Uncle Paul said again in a perfect imitation of how my mother would have sounded yelling to Patty in her driveway.

My mother and Patty had never shared more than a quick sentence or two of conversation. My grandma Anna had told my mom to trust only your family, and to beware of what she called "coffee klatches." My mother dutifully did so, not that I recall her being invited to any. But when Mom was walking to church or the local convenience store, she would stop and converse with Mrs. Matthews and Mrs. Kevorkian who lived down the street.

Patty was another story. Even as a child I sensed that Patty had a detached, almost distracted quality about her. Truth be told, Mom didn't care for Patty. Mom didn't like the fact that she had given up custody of her two young children from her first marriage years ago to marry Buddy. Even more, Mom didn't like the fact that while Patty always gave my mom a chilly reception, she would always smile and exchange a remark or two with my dad when they crossed paths at our intersecting walkways. And yet, somehow, Mom knew all about Patty's husband's affair and new girlfriend. I wasn't shocked. Many people confided their troubles to my mom, and, despite their nonexistent relationship, Patty was no exception.

"Josephine, how could you?" my uncle continued as his tone became serious. "Patty has to be in her forties, and the new girlfriend is—what—twenty? And gorgeous, I might add."

My mother rolled her eyes, and someone, perhaps the ever-kind Aunt Gladys, changed the subject. But I was left feeling that Uncle Paul was right. My mother was strong in her convictions and often said that she could "feel it in her bones." But even I could tell there was no way the man next door was coming back. Was she just being kind, or was she trying to get Patty off Dad's trail? In my chair by the ocean, I was once again pondering this mystery when Mom said something that really caught my attention.

"And all those hours I spent alone when you worked the night shift," she said angrily to my dad.

Uh oh, this was a sore point. Dad didn't react right away, which wasn't unusual. But he looked pale, which was. My dad was known for his high and somewhat ruddy coloring, which had the effect of making him look at least ten years younger. His color had drained, and I decided it was high time we moved back into the somewhat cooler apartment. But before I could make a move, Dad made a declaration that almost knocked me out of my chair.

"You know, I never had to work the night shift," he said matter-of-factly.

What? I screamed in my head.

"*Whaaaaaaat?*" Mom screamed out loud.

My dad worked the night shift at the Hostess cake factory—first in Hoboken, then in East Brunswick—from before I was born until he retired at the age of sixty-two in 1979 when I was a junior in college. Our lives revolved around Dad's night shift work. From "no yelling" during the day in the apartment at 809 New York Avenue where I played as a child to Mom always sending me out of the house to play during my grammar school days in Ridgefield Park, the night shift was a hardship. Dad's night shift work impacted us in a very negative way. Well, apparently not *all* of us.

Mom collected herself before I could even react. "What do you *mean,* you didn't have to work the night shift?" Her eyes were bulging, and she was gripping the arms of her folding chair.

Dad was nonplussed. "The foreman on the day shift never liked me and I never liked him," Dad replied.

"That's it?" Mom replied. "That's the reason?"

She seemed like she wanted to say more, and then she stopped. I could have filled in the blanks for her. As in, that was the reason we suffered all those years? But confronting my dad on a big issue was just something Mom and I never did. Ever. I learned from her to let things slide. Sure, my parents had their small quibbles from time to time. But an explosive argument over a large issue, such as my dad's drinking, rarely happened.

We sat in silence for a moment until something caught my mom's eye. It was the yarn sitting in my lap.

"What color is that yarn?" she asked abruptly.

To be fair, I was not in the best frame of mind. My brain told me the yarn was a greenish turquoise, but my mouth said something else.

"Blue," I answered.

"Blue!" my mother shouted. "It's green!"

I was about to agree when I noticed a group of students from nearby Monmouth University standing nearby. They had most likely been making their way from their apartment to the beach when they noticed the spectacle taking place on the "village green" of the apartment complex.

I glanced at the students, hoping they would start walking away, when my mother yelled, "Blue? What makes you think it's blue? Are you blind?"

Now I was truly mortified. "Mother!" I huffed in response, praying that none of the gathered students was visually impaired or knew someone who was.

The students continued to stand in place and stare at us, mouths agape. I half wondered if they hoped they had stumbled upon a live performance staged for them by the university. After all, my parents' apartment complex was being transitioned into student housing. Maybe they thought this was a "Theater on the Green" version of *Grey Gardens*. Mom and I were certainly acting the parts. Of course, Dad was a wild card. Where does the good-looking older gentleman fit in? they may have wondered. I swear if I had stripped down to my skivvies and done the flag dance, à la Little Edie Bouvier, the student onlookers would not have been surprised.

"It's green, okay?" I hissed at Mom. The students were still watching, wide-eyed. I was embarrassed, but also proud. If nothing else, my parents and I had a wow factor.

"If you say so," Mom said with a doubtful grimace.

"Let's call it a day and settle on turquoise," I said, lifting Dad up from his chair. "It's time to go inside."

"Already?" Dad said. Oh, to be Dad. The seemingly clueless man who never enters the fray and always appears as regal as a viscount.

I didn't stay long after that. I couldn't decide who to be more upset with at that point. Mom, for suddenly turning on me like a rottweiler? Or Dad, for upending our lives all those years ago for his own comfort? The students moved on, finally, and I managed the task of depositing Dad into his armchair. He settled in, and I made my move to leave my parents to their own devices once again. Dad called out to me before I shut the apartment door on my way out.

"Don't be a stranger," he said, and I could hear worry in his voice. Maybe he wasn't so clueless after all.

"I won't," I promised, and I felt my anger softening.

How many times, I wondered on the drive home, had Mom found a bone to pick with me when she was in fact upset with my dad? My mother eventually gave up on changing any of Dad's traits, including his stubbornness. Instead she turned toward me and pinned most of her hopes and dreams there. I could almost feel them at times, flying off of her like small sparkling gems and landing on me with a thud. "Be a cheerleader, you've got the legs for it! You're so smart, you can be whatever you want!" Mom's constant faith in me made me sparkle like glitter. But it wasn't all positive. Had she ever before tossed her anger onto me, as she had on this day? I thought hard about this and realized she had. Because my dad was prone to depression, I was never allowed to be sad. Because my dad was a beer drinker, I was told that a lady never sits at a bar. I could go on, but there's no point. Because on that day, I also realized something else. Somehow it was all okay.

When you grow up with a combat veteran for your dad, you come to understand a lot. Even if you don't want to.

It's not easy to live life as a veteran, keeping secrets and hiding emotional scars while the rest of the world hums along as though nothing happened.

It's also not easy to be the wife of a veteran. It requires a lot of courage and perspective and wisdom and maturity. And, in Mom's case at least, some disappointment.

My mom may not have realized all that she was getting into when she married my dad. But she was well-equipped for it. She was tough as nails. She got us all through it. I'd be a fool to complain about that.

Weeks later, I handed my friend Leslie that crocheted scarf. "I love the color," she said. She looked confused when I started to laugh, and I asked her if she thought it was blue or green.

Chapter Fourteen

My Father Has Fallen and I Can't Get Up!

ONE WARM EVENING IN 2012, DAD MANAGED TO DO WHAT I had feared for years. Even worse, it was my fault. Before my mother could stop him, he stood up from his armchair to answer the door.

They had expected me fifteen minutes prior, but I was running late, as was my terrible habit. The strong wind off of the ocean must have triggered a noise, and because he was expecting my arrival, he mistook the noise for a knock. He ended up tripping on a throw rug that I had meant to tell my mother to pick up during my last visit. I had forgotten.

It was John who received the call from my mom. He immediately called 911 for an ambulance and raced to the hospital, where he arrived before I did. Alerted by his text message, I turned around two blocks from their apartment and headed to the emergency room of the nearest hospital.

Dad was in bad shape, with a concussion and a head wound that required stitches, but luckily no broken bones. I cursed myself for buying him a twenty-four-pack of beer just the day before. I knew drinking had most likely led to this. At the office of Dad's primary care physician, my mother routinely answered the question "how many drinks does he have a day?" with "one or two." I would sit there passively, silently swearing but feeling powerless to argue. Mom was the one dealing with him, not me. He was living under her roof, not mine. If beer made him happy, and most likely made him easier for her to deal with, who was I to argue?

But this time, something in me snapped when the attending nurse asked if my father had had alcohol that day. I finally got the nerve to speak up.

"He's drinking three or four cans a day," I said, doing some quick math. I knew I bought him a twenty-four-pack about once a week.

"That's too many at his age, and especially for the medication he's on for the prostate cancer," the nurse said. "We're going to have to detox him." I felt my knees go weak. My mind flashed back to something my mother had told me years ago. After spending years on the front lines in World War II, my dad contracted malaria during the African campaign. He recovered enough to be sent back into the service, but it was decided that he would not return to the battlefield in the same capacity. He was placed in the ambulance service, which might have seemed like a godsend. It was, and it wasn't. The ambulance driver my dad was assigned to turned out to be a drinker who encouraged him to drink as well. Once again, I cursed the fates that had sapped my father's potential and spirit.

My mother seemed not to have heard the conversation between me and the nurse, thank goodness. I feared she would intervene. But she did not, and what I had hoped would happen for a few years could finally took place. Because of the blood thinners and his pacemaker, my dad ended up in the hospital's heart ward. It was there that, at the age of ninety-four, he was detoxed using an intravenous method.

Dad's next stop was a rehabilitation facility, which was sparkling clean and staffed with basically the nicest people on the planet. They all loved my affable dad, who thank-you'd them all to the nth degree. He even befriended his much younger roommate, once again proving that curmudgeon and charisma can indeed exist peacefully in the same frail body.

But it soon became apparent that the concussion had put Dad in a highly confused state. From his conversations with us, we learned that he believed he was being cared for in a large house by a lovely woman and her large family consisting of mostly girls (aka the nurses) in another country during World War II. He recognized me, my mom, and other family members, but he believed we were all visitors to this woman's home. This led to great consternation on my part. One day I began to cry while driving my mother home because I feared my dad would never snap out of it.

I expected her to commiserate. But I had forgotten how strong and smart she could be.

"Don't be ridiculous, he's going to be fine," she told me. "Now stop crying and keep driving."

But even Mom was given pause when she took the rehabilitation center's staff up on an offer. For a low cost, she could order a meal and eat with Dad. She expected him to be pleased, but he was horrified.

"What!" he cried, uncharacteristically raising his voice. "You expect this poor woman to cook for you, too?"

In the end, Dad came to his senses again. We returned him to his small apartment by the sea, to once again be cared for by the woman he loved, adored by his grandchildren, and cherished by his immediate and extended family. The Dad I saw after that was good-humored, sharp, and patient, and not much different than the Dad I had before detox. But he lacked an edge and the negative comments he sometimes shared about others when we were alone. In other words, he was the new and improved version of Dad. I regretted not taking action sooner. My children were finally enjoying the Grampy they should have had all along. Some of our happiest memories occurred during the last year of Dad's life, whether we were taking him to his favorite place (Atlantic City) or just sitting on my back deck and talking about the good old days.

In the last year of his life, Dad was happy. Dad was carefree. And Dad, to my amazement, had light shining in his eyes.

Finally.

Chapter Fifteen

Dragons Live Forever

DAD ENDURED OVER THREE YEARS OF MONTHLY ROUNDS of injections into his stomach to curb the prostate cancer (after which he thanked the nurse and told her she had done a wonderful job and he hadn't felt a thing, every single time, while Mom and I stared at the floor and winced). Knowing that his time could be limited, I made it a point to get him out for his coffee and doughnut and to his beloved slot machines as often as I could.

And then, just a few days after a marvelous day trip to Atlantic City with Mom, John, me, and my cousin Lois, Dad died in his sleep. "Dragons live forever, but not so little boys," was the first thought that came into my head. Dad had outlived many of his contemporaries, and my close friends and family members had sometimes joked that he would live forever. Of course, we all knew better. And by the time he passed, I knew that living forever was the last thing Dad wanted. He seemed to sense the strain Mom was under and that his care had gotten beyond her.

Dad would not have wanted a big fuss made over his passing, and I was more than happy to comply. I was numb and, frankly, relieved. Dad had been losing his ability to walk and would have needed either a nursing home or twenty-four-hour nursing care. It would have been tough on us, but horrible for Dad. He had only acquiesced to using a wheelchair a few months earlier, preferring the "human chain" of helping hands from me, Mom, and John. We decided on an intimate afternoon memorial at my home for close family and friends. This would be followed by a brief visitation at the funeral home and burial at a nearby veteran's cemetery.

I knew Dad would have been pleased with the lightness surrounding his passing. Like the rest of us, Dad endured the all-too-early loss of John's parents to cancer. John and I were blessed in that Jo and Joe and Dolly and Otto made a jolly little crew. I recall Mom telling me years before that I was fortunate John's parents were relatively young because they would be around a long time for my kids. And then cancer pulled the rug out from under us. Dolly passed away at the age of sixty-two in 1995, when Greg was a year and a half and Veronica was less than a year. Otto passed away five years later. After Otto's service, my dad said, "No more." And I knew what he meant.

"No more wakes," I said, just to clarify. "Not even your own?"

"*Especially* not my own," he said.

After the viewing for Dad at the funeral home, Mom, John, Veronica, and I were in the parking lot preparing for the trip to the veteran's cemetery. We watched as the chauffeur of the hearse bearing Dad's coffin exited the funeral home and opened the driver's-side door. She was a tall and beautiful blonde wearing a navy blue skirt and blazer. Knee-high boots accentuated her long and shapely legs, and a cap balanced almost jauntily atop her perfectly coiffed platinum locks.

I said what Mom and John were surely thinking: "Just Dad's type."

And then all of us did one of Dad's favorite things. We laughed at our own joke.

It was always about Dad, ever since I can remember. "Promise me you'll never put him in a nursing home," Mom said about two years before he passed. Being a dutiful only daughter, I promised. A few months later, I made a request of my mother. "Promise me you won't die before he does," I said.

I was relieved but not surprised that Mom was unoffended by my request. She loved my dad deeply, but she knew he could be a handful. "I promise," Mom said.

As usual, she was true to her word. And then some.

I used to believe that when someone lives to be ninety-five, you should celebrate their longevity and not concern yourself overly much with mourning their passing. John and I and our children pushed down a lot of sadness, telling ourselves that we were lucky to have had Dad around for so long. Then, in the summer of 2015, more than two years later, the grief came rushing at me in waves. I missed my dad's smile. I missed his humor. I missed his blue eyes, the likes of which I haven't seen since. I missed his silent but reassuring presence. And on the rare occasions when we took Mom out someplace, I despised being a trio and no longer a quartet. I realized that both John and I could use closure regarding Dad's passing. We'd kept it light, but perhaps too light. We had never really mourned my dad the way we were meant to. I had an idea.

I had thought I would never want to see my parents' former apartment after dragging so many black plastic garbage bags out of it. But I convinced John that I was ready, so, on a mid-August evening, we headed to the rooftop of the Windmill restaurant across the street from the apartment. We ate our hot dogs (which Dad ordered as "wienies" whenever we brought him there, much to John's embarrassment) and gazed at Mom and Dad's former place across the street. We talked about our memories. The four of us taking the kids for a walk on the beach or watching as they kicked a soccer ball back and forth along the grassy path between the beach and the apartment. Me searching for sea glass with Veronica as the sun was setting, and Dad and John watching from the boardwalk.

Once, when my father still had his "walking legs," he and John took an after-dinner stroll and didn't return for over an hour. They'd walked to Pier Village and back while my mother fretted.

"I'm fine," Dad told her upon their return, clearly annoyed.

We had made the most of that little apartment by the sea. On warm summer nights we would walk to the pizza parlor, the ice cream shop, and, of course, the food store. If we were lucky, a visit from Aunt Millie and my cousins would cap the evening off and provide memories and laughs.

As John and I polished off the last of our cheese fries and prepared to leave for a quick stroll on the nearby boardwalk, I had to ask the burning question.

"Do you ever regret my parents paying years of rent and running out of money?"

John's gaze fell across the small back windows of the apartment that held so many years of shining moments. It was where we would arrive to fetch Mom and Dad for a day trip to Atlantic City and where Dad would give us each some of his gambling money and wish us good luck. It was where Dad would sit in his armchair and look out of the large floor-to-ceiling window at ships, sailboats, and passersby. We'd once set up a model train on a table that took up most of the living room in the apartment and kept it there for three years. And the apartment was where we arrived one summer evening with my then-teenage son Greg and his best friend in tow. It was a few days after I had confided in Mom that the young man, having seen my mom embrace Greg, told me had never been hugged by any of his grandparents.

"Come here," Mom said to Greg's friend as we were preparing to leave. "I'm going to give you a hug." And she did, as my heart swelled with pride and my eyes filled with tears.

I could see the light of memories in John's eyes along with the reflection of the sun setting beyond the ocean.

"No," John said. "I don't regret a thing."

"Me either," I said. And, for the first time, I felt like I meant it.

Chapter Sixteen

Spoiled Rotten, or Just Overripe?

WHEN I WAS FOUR YEARS OLD, MY SECURE LITTLE WORLD was rocked by an innocent query from my beautiful young mother. And I responded in a way that would surprise no one who knows me well.

One day, as we headed into the lobby of our apartment building at 809 New York Avenue, my mother casually asked me if I would like a baby brother or sister. Thinking she must be having one imminently, as most four-year-olds would, I blew a gasket. I'm talking all-out hissy fit. My mother half carried me up the three long flights to our small but beautifully decorated apartment as I screamed and carried on, flailing my feet and lashing out with my small fists. I remember the event well, with embarrassment, but what stands out most in my mind is the fact that doors on every floor opened with curious faces behind them. Had I been just any child having a meltdown, those faces might have shown a flash of anger. But what I recall was seeing kind and concerned faces and hearing, "Oh, poor Mary Ann, what's wrong?" during our trek up three flights of stairs.

My mother was too embarrassed and overwhelmed to speak. I don't even recall her apologizing to our fellow tenants. Perhaps there was no need to. My family was well-known and well-loved throughout the building. My parents made a handsome couple and had lived in the building for thirteen years, beginning in 1950. (I was born in 1958, nine years after my parents' marriage—Mom was thirty-one, Dad forty-two). The building's flinty, chain-smoking superintendent kept the whole place sparkling and running. She took her job so seriously, she once delivered a right-hook punch to the face of belligerent tenant who refused to rinse out her milk bottles before placing them in the hallway for pickup and refill.

The long-term tenants could recall an incident that had happened a few years before I was born and were most likely relieved that my parents stayed together and managed to have a child. There had been a fire in the embroidery factory next door, and my mother had been told by the apartment building's superintendent to evacuate. Not seeing a lot of smoke and thinking the factory was far enough away that the fire wouldn't take hold of our apartment building, she did what she thought was the right thing. She grabbed the cage of my father's beloved parakeet, Tippy, and brought the bird downstairs and out of the building without disturbing my father from his pre-work-shift nap. Less than fifteen minutes later, my father awoke to the sound of firemen standing on the fire escape and rapping at the window, laughing at him as he approached them from bed wearing just his skivvies.

"Get out, get out!" they yelled. In his retelling of the story, which happened often, Dad claimed that he frantically scoured the apartment in search of my mother and his beloved parakeet (who was, by all accounts, one heck of a bird). When he came up empty, he scrambled down the stairs and through the marble lobby to encounter all of the tenants—including my mother, holding a cage containing Tippy.

"You left me in there!" he said loudly (my father never yelled).

"Well, they said not to worry . . . and the parakeet's lungs are so tiny," my mother said defensively, much to the amusement of the crowd.

I don't know that my father ever trusted my mom fully after that, and I can't say I blame him. That being said, Mom was right. The fire never did spread to our building. Dad, however, never forgave her.

"They laughed at me," Dad would say, shaking his head as Mom rolled her eyes. In retrospect, my dad most likely wished he had stayed in bed and taken his chances. He was an extremely private person, and the thought of strangers seeing him in his boxers—and laughing, no less—haunted him to the end of his days.

By the way, rumor has it that the embroidery factory fire was started by a chain-smoker with a mean right hook who worked there part time.

My early childhood was mostly idyllic, with the three-story walkup holding me in its warm embrace. My three older cousins lived in the same building, and we played together often. I enjoyed frequent walks to the park and the nearby candy store owned by Aunt Rosanna and Uncle Lou. I was a princess in a magical kingdom made of bricks and steel and hope and love.

But nothing lasts forever.

My mom's sister Millie and her family, including my grandma Anna, left Union City in 1962. This move took away my mom's two best friends—her sister and her mom—and my favorite three playmates. We were devastated. But we understood.

My cousin Barbara, Aunt Millie's then-nine-year-old daughter, had been hit by a car while playing in front of our building. Barbara stepped off the curb just as a sedan driven by a young woman veered toward the sidewalk. Barbara ended up with broken ribs and a short hospital stay. Her father, my uncle Sal, incensed that the young woman was not arrested because she was the daughter of a judge in a politically corrupt system, decided to move his family out of Hudson County. They left in 1962, heading for a brand new home in a town my Uncle Sal had heard about. Their new destination of Jackson, New Jersey, was over an hour and a half away from Union City. My mom, as was her habit, did her best to fill the void left by the loss of her sister and mom. Not surprisingly, it involved children. My mom adored children, but was blessed with just one. Although in later years she professed that she saw this as God's will, her actions around that time say otherwise.

My mother would try and fail to adopt two siblings for me in 1962 and 1963. One was Bobby, a playmate around my age who often traveled with Mom and me to "the Avenue," as in Bergenline Avenue. Bergenline Avenue was *the* shopping area in our part of Hudson County, stretching a few miles through Union City and West New York. Mom would pull a red wagon with Bobby and me in it the full six blocks to Bergenline Avenue, which was for our family the harbinger of all things beautiful, including pastries, Italian ices, meats, vegetables for dinner, and—most importantly—toy shopping and hot chocolate with whipped cream at the Woolworth's.

I recall Bobby as fun, respectful, and kind. He was around my age, maybe a year or so older. My mother claims that we even looked alike, though I can't recall or find any photos of him. When his mother passed away in early 1963, Mom had thoughts of approaching Bobby's father—who was apparently overwhelmed by the care of Bobby and his brothers—to see if we could "take Bobby off his hands." Within days, though, Bobby came to visit and told us that he and his brothers were being adopted by his aunt. My mother was happy for Bobby and his brothers, but I could see that she was heartbroken.

Next in line was Maria, the daughter of a Cuban immigrant mother. Maria was older than I was, perhaps nine, but in appearance and manners seemed like a teenager. Newly arrived to the U.S., Maria was brilliant and had picked up English quickly and amazingly well. She was stunningly beautiful and funny and I desperately wanted her to be the big sister I could look up to. Although I don't know the details, Maria's mother put the kibosh on my mother's offer to take Maria off her hands. Year later, Mom told me that Maria's mother worked as a prostitute, further breaking my heart.

Mom became frustrated and sad, and it must have been a lonely time for her. She was accustomed to heading downstairs for coffee with her family, or taking my Grandma Anna shopping on the avenue. Given the chance, she would surely have been more socially connected. But my dad preferred to sit in his favorite chair, nursing a beer or two and then heading off to bed before his next shift at the factory. Mom began to complain about the money he spent on beer, and the times he headed to the bar with friends after his shift ended. To be fair, I never saw my father inebriated. But for my mother, who grew up with a grandfather who drank to excess and became verbally abusive, it must have been unsettling to realize that she couldn't change the fact that my dad drank beer every day. Dad turned a deaf ear to Mom's complaints. In retrospect, I am certain that their apartment began to feel like a prison to her.

In the summer of 1964, after I had completed kindergarten, my mother made a last stab at life in Union City. We were running out of room in our one-bedroom apartment (apartment 3D, just like in *I Love Lucy*). With a thought toward finally giving me my own bedroom, or perhaps with hopes of somehow procuring more children to raise, Mom brought me to look at the bottom floor of a two-family home for rent. By that time, the influx of immigrants from Cuba was bringing changes to Union City. Mom and I welcomed the diversity and the chance to meet new people. I befriended a shy Cuban girl named Pilar, and we were looking forward to our next year at St. Anthony's grammar school.

Mom and I walked the few blocks down Thirty-Second Street toward the complex that included St. Anthony's Church and grammar school. I remember feeling pleased that the apartment for rent was located right across from my school, which I loved. But when my mother pushed the buzzer to speak with the owner of the house, it became immediately clear that this person spoke only Spanish. My mother attempted to communicate using English, until the woman actually opened up an upstairs window and yelled at us to "Go away!" I can't recall whether she used Spanish or English for this communication, but either way we got the point.

We were shocked. I saw a defeated look on Mom's face, and I knew in a heartbeat that we would be leaving Union City. Blinking away tears, I looked across the street at the orange brick façade of my beloved school and church. I doubted life could be as good anywhere else.

And then a miracle happened. My aunt Bernice stepped in.

Aunt Bernice adored her brother Joe and convinced my parents to move to the town where she had settled, a half hour away. My dad was an easy sell, but my non-driving mother not so much. My wise Aunt Bernice told her, privately, that—unlike Union City—her town did not have a bar on almost every corner. Mom was sold.

A bucolic and tree-filled village located in close proximity to New York City, Ridgefield Park, New Jersey, is best known for hosting the largest and longest-running Fourth of July parade in our country's history. Ridgefield Park is also the birthplace of Ozzie Nelson, an American band leader who originated and starred in *The Adventures of Ozzie and Harriet*. This long-running television series featured Ozzie, his wife Harriet, and their sons

David and Ricky Nelson. Ozzie and Harriet were "as American as apple pie" and did a lot to bolster Ridgefield Park's status.

Aunt Bernice had convinced my parents that Ridgefield Park was the perfect place to raise a family. It was conveniently located a half hour away from Dad and Bernice's two other sisters—Betty, who lived in Emerson, and Gladys, who lived in Jersey City. I was still doubtful, yearning for the days when my aunt Millie's family and my beloved grandma Anna, as well as my mom's uncle Lou and aunt Rosanna, lived in the same building.

Then, shortly after we decided to make the move to Ridgefield Park, I overheard my aunt Bernice telling my parents a fascinating story.

"I was feeding the squirrels in my front yard, and a woman from the neighborhood walked right up to me in the driveway," Aunt Bernice related, red-faced. "And she said, 'We always spot you city slickers a mile away because you are the only ones who feed squirrels. After all, *we* know they're only rats with fluffy tails.'"

"What did you *say* to her?" my mother asked.

"Well, I told her to get off of my property and never come back and to mind her own business from now on."

My dad laughed, my mom looked shocked, and my aunt looked mighty pleased.

I was intrigued. I didn't know much about Ridgefield Park. I knew a lot about Union City. I had spent hours playing in its large leafy parks and in the small plot of dirt behind our apartment with my cousins. I had nestled my cheek into the large flowers on my grandmother's dresses as we sat together in our pew at St. Anthony's Church. I had greeted residents of our apartment building when entering its sparkling marble lobby and received candy and coins from them. I had been babysat by Mrs. Gassman who lived in the apartment across the hall and been brought dinner on a tray by her as I lounged and watched TV. I had sat on the flat tar roof of our apartment building in a webbed lawn chair while my dad and my mother's brother Mike—who lived in the apartment building next door—watched a baseball game on a portable TV. I had bought fancy but scratchy dresses at the Mickey Finn's discount store on Bergenline Avenue with Mom and enjoyed egg creams at the nearby soda fountain countless times with Dad. Union City, with its brownstones and grit and its view of New York City, had gotten under my skin. I doubted that Ridgefield Park could ever do the same. But Aunt Bernice's story about her neighbor had given me hope that it might.

I could already tell that arriving in Ridgefield Park on the coattails of my feisty, funny aunt could prove to be entertainment of the highest order.

As it turns out, I was correct in that assumption. Within weeks, in the summer of 1964, we were settled nicely into our spacious apartment on the top floor of Sixty-Two Overpeck Avenue.

My aunt Bernice did not have to work too hard to find us a rental. Sixty-Two Overpeck just happened to be the house next door to hers.

Chapter Seventeen

Sixty-Eight Overlook

IN THE FALL OF 1964, MY PARENTS BOUGHT THEIR FIRST—and last—home at Sixty-Eight Overlook Avenue, after living in the top floor of the house next door to Aunt Bernice for a year. Sixty-Eight Overlook Avenue was a somewhat dilapidated bungalow located on a dead-end street at the bottom of a steep hill. But it had good bones, a spacious backyard, an expansive view of the New Jersey meadowlands, and the blessing of its former owner, Mr. Schultz. I recall Mr. Schultz as a tall and friendly white-haired man, who was thrilled to have a young family moving in. "My wife loved this house, she even died in it," Mr. Schultz told my mom as she took the keys. For the one time in her life that I can recall, my mom had no words.

Grandma Anna, who was living with my aunt Millie's family in their brand-new and spacious split-level home in Jackson, offered her opinion upon seeing the home.

"You should maybe tear it down and start again," she said.

Her feelings hurt and her confidence shattered, Mom turned an even more critical eye toward the small and somewhat ramshackle bungalow.

But Mom and Grandma had forgotten the first rule of real estate. Location, location, location.

Sixty-Eight Overlook Avenue was located within walking distance of Aunt Bernice and Uncle Paul's house. Visitors were always welcome at Aunt Bernice's dark green Victorian-style home at Fifty-Six Overpeck Avenue. The home, with its huge wraparound porch and view of the meadows, was the scene of many boisterous gatherings filled with uncles, aunts, cousins, and friends. But my favorite holiday was the Fourth of July.

Ours was a very patriotic family, and my father and my aunts' husbands were all veterans. Aunt Bernice was born on the fifth of July, so we celebrated not only Independence Day, but the almost-birthday of everyone's favorite aunt.

The great time we had on the Fourth of July included the morning parade and later the evening fireworks display in Veteran's Park. We filled the afternoon by splashing in the above-ground pool (kids) or enjoying a cocktail or soda on the pool's deck (adults). Everyone enjoyed Uncle Paul's grilled hot dogs and hamburgers along with his homemade macaroni salad. ("No mayo, folks, bad for the ticker," he would announce.)

It was always a memorable and wonderful experience, and one that for many of us has never been equaled. Aunt Bernice and Uncle Paul, although inundated with guests, were the most relaxed hosts imaginable. One of the best Independence Day memories I have is when my aunt's neighbor Ty Brewster, who had actually cut a vinyl record of himself singing "God Bless America," climbed onto his roof and belted out the song for the benefit of the entire neighborhood. I remember all of us stopping whatever game we were playing at that moment in the pool and applauding wildly at the conclusion. My aunt Bernice always shared her belief that "nobody sings that song like Kate Smith." On that day, Ty Brewster was named a close second.

When discussing our childhoods in Ridgefield Park, my longtime friends and I often say that the village had a way of getting into your blood. I can still close my eyes and feel the cool slate sidewalks under my feet as I walk past an assortment of large colonial homes, most containing an assortment of family members. As an only child, I was an anomaly in Ridgefield Park. Luckily, as I had in Union City, I stumbled into an extended family that held me close. In Union City, I was spoiled. In Ridgefield Park, I was schooled. My smarmy "me-first" self was thrown into a circus-like atmosphere of cousins who were by and large smarter, funnier, more attractive, and more popular than I was. And I fell in love with every single one of them.

Of course, telling any one of them, or any of my aunts, for that matter, was verboten. My father's family never told you they loved you. What was the point, really, when you were more than likely to see one another again so soon—if not in the space of a week, then surely a month? The Mandrick group enjoyed one another's company and never spent too much time apart. This family togetherness never felt smothering and was a bedrock in times of trouble. When I was feeling the sting of loneliness just before entering high school, having few friends and experiencing few social gatherings, I could always find security and a good time in the company of my aunts, uncles, and cousins.

There were family excursions, as often and as far as our tight budgets would allow. Palisades Amusement Park. Keansburg. Crestwood Lake. Snipes in Secaucus. Point Pleasant, if we were lucky. Our entire family once took a road trip to the newly opened Vince Lombardi service area on the New Jersey Turnpike, fifteen minutes away. Just because.

When we were together, everything was fun. An onlooker might have assumed, upon seeing our family in action, that we had been somehow blessed with endless resources. Nothing could have been further from the truth. The family elders worked hard to make things happen and were often employed in more than one job at a time. Uncle Paul, for example, worked as a bartender in the evenings in addition to his full-time job at

Sun Chemical Company. Aunt Betty held a host of part-time gigs in addition to raising her children—including assembling dollhouses for the famous FAO Schwartz toy store. I can still recall my grandpa Joe, my father's imposing six-foot-three figure of a dad, spray-painting tiny wooden posts that my aunt would use to assemble staircases in the dollhouses. My dad worked the night shift at the Hostess cake factory for years. Aunt Gladys worked full-time while raising three children. Yet I don't recall anyone complaining about being tired or overwhelmed.

Under the tutelage of the Mandricks, both my mother and I came into our own. We grew up. As painful as it was to leave behind family members in Union City—and to lose my aunt Millie's family to their new home in Jackson—I now realize it needed to happen.

Mom became an integral part of the goings-on, an accepted member of the troupe. Sure, she still had her moments and missed her sister Millie terribly. Yet by the time my parents sold their home in 2002, a love of their little house and almost all things Ridgefield Park coursed through their veins.

Out from under the watchful eyes of her family in Union City, Mom shed some of the many fears she was known for and became more adventurous. She never swam or rode a bicycle, mind you, but she allowed me to do so. I do, however, recall one frightening incident that occurred when Mom offered to babysit Bernice and Paul's children, Nancy and Bob. I was seven years old at the time. Ten-year-old Bob and four-year-old Nancy begged to play a game of hide and seek, and Mom agreed.

"No hiding in the closets," she said, fearing our suffocation. I am serious.

Long story short, Bob discovered a clever hiding place that had nothing to do with closets. We eventually found him on the roof when he tired of hiding and began yelling out to us. Fortunately, it was a lesser roof outside of his bedroom in my aunt's

Victorian-style home. It was a mere twenty or so feet from the ground. My white-faced mother helped us drag him back into the house through a window.

"You said no closets, not no roofs," Bob informed my mother calmly after her panic attack subsided. As if *she* was the perpetrator.

"That Bob," she said to Dad later over dinner.

"That Bob," he responded, and not for the last time.

But then Mom surprised us by laughing about it. And it wouldn't be the last time that a member of the somewhat free-wheeling Mandrick clan would teach her the lesson of "all's well that ends well."

After that incident, or perhaps despite it, Mom began to relax. She transformed the dingy bungalow into a warm gathering spot, doing the best she could to work with its rustic charms. My friends and cousins remember a tiny and spotless home with coffee, tea, and other refreshments always at the ready. No one was allowed to leave the house without eating or drinking *something*. A beer or soda offered by Dad, perhaps, or coffee and cookies and a sandwich offered by Mom. My mother, never a willing hostess in her Union City days due to her nervousness and lack of space, entertained the Mandrick family casually and often. They were a no-frills, no-nonsense group that put every hostess at ease.

In 1978, John was introduced to my father's side of the family as my first steady boyfriend. John was both dazzled and terrified. My aunts', uncles', and cousins' reputations preceded them, thanks to tales I had told him. My alternately hilarious and no-nonsense aunt Bernice had once phoned a large car dealership in nearby Hackensack, infuriated that they were flying a large American flag at night without shining a light on it (the manager immediately complied and thanked her). Bernice's husband Paul was a larger-than-life teller of stories and a spot-on mimic.

Although you couldn't help but laugh at his outrageous tales, you would be wise to fly under his radar lest you become his latest victim. My cousin Bob was the family jokester, having inherited his parents' senses of fun and humor. Immediately upon meeting John, who had a square jaw and wore glasses and worked as a reporter, Bob dubbed him "Clark Kent."

"Clark is here," Bob would announce when John arrived at family gatherings. John would smile and wince at the same time. Deep down, he was glad to be a part of the shenanigans.

To my relief and his, the entire group took to John right away and included him in the fun, which included regaling him with tales of our family's brushes with fame. (My great-uncle Jack DeMave was a boxer once known as the "Golden Boy of Hoboken"; his son Jack starred in the TV show *Lassie* and appeared on many other shows, including *The Mary Tyler Moore Show*; Jack's sister Jacqueline was a producer on *Good Morning America*; and, last but not least, Aunt Betty's boss, always referred to as "Mr. Newman," was George W. Newman—known for his outdoor advertising empire Allied Advertising and instrumental in financing the creation of the Secaucus Junction train station.)

I was proud of the Mandricks and knew I was lucky to be a part of the action.

My three aunts reminded me of the three fairy godmothers in *Sleeping Beauty*, who each had a gift to bestow.

Aunt Gladys had the gift of style.

Aunt Bernice had the gift of fun.

Aunt Betty had the gift of generosity.

And my mom, Aunt Josephine, added the gift of warmth.

Perhaps the best thing about moving to Ridgefield Park was seeing the change that came over my mom. She was no longer fixated on adopting a child or moving to Jackson to be with her sister and mother. Her quest for perfection, or at least improvement, was still there. It just wasn't as sharp and pointy. Time spent with my father's family and her down-to-earth neighbors softened my mother and made her a part of the fabric. Mom might have hated that dilapidated bungalow on sight, but in reality she belonged there. In the 1970s, my parents added a beautiful redwood deck to the back of the house. It became a gathering place for assorted family members and friends through the years. It was on that deck that, as a teenager, I overheard part of a conversation between my mom and my aunt Bernice.

"Don't worry about what you want, Josephine," my aunt said on that sunny day. "Just treasure what you have."

Aunt Millie and Mom.

Aunt Millie, Uncle Gabe, and Mom.

My mom Josephine and her sister Millie as teenagers in Union City.

My dad Joe Mandrick Jr., his sister Gladys, and my grandmother Jeanette watching a parade in Hoboken.

Joe Mandrick, Jr. and Joe Mandrick, Sr. in June 1941.

Clockwise from left: my great-grandmother Jeanette, Dad, Mom, Aunt Millie, Uncle Tim, Uncle Gabe, Grandma Anna, Uncle Mike, and great-grandmother Josephine.

Mom doing her best to dress like a country girl.

Dad and a friendly cow embracing the pastoral life.

Mom with my cousin Barbara in Union City.

Dad, me, and Tippy the amazing parakeet.

Mom and me.   Me and Mom.

With my doll on Christmas Day 1962.

My best friend Pilar and me at Kindergarten Graduation, St. Anthony's School in Union City, Spring 1963.

Me and my cousin Bob, Easter 1964 in Ridgefield Park. Aunt Bernice's Fiat is to the left of us.

Mom and me in our Easter finest, posing in the backyard of 68 Overlook Avenue.

My cousins Patricia and Michael, and my cousin Betty Jean *(left to right)* and me and my Grandma Anna when she lived with us.

Dad and his beloved Ford Maverick, with 68 Overlook Avenue in the background.

Dad, Mom, me, John, and John's parents Dolly and Otto on our wedding day in June 1983.

A Mandrick family gathering—Uncle Halsey, Aunt Betty, Aunt Bernice, me, Mom, cousin Tom, Aunt Gladys, Dad, Uncle Fred, Uncle Paul, and cousin Nancy.

John making a toast to Mom on her 80th birthday in 2007.

Dad with my Uncle Mike and Uncle Gabe *(left to right)* at a family reunion in 1990.

Dancing at my niece's wedding.

Mom and Aunt Millie in church.

Chapter Eighteen

Trouble on the Rails

DEMENTIA WASN'T THE FIRST EVENT TO COME ALONG AND take something away from my mother. She endured a childhood that started out promising and turned as sour as the grapes her grandfather used to make homemade wine. Her Italian immigrant parents, Anna Mastrangelo and William D'Annunzio, were madly in love and had four children in the space of the six years they were married. They were raising their family in a six-family apartment building on Thirty-Second Street in Union City, New Jersey. William, a vegetarian and a believer in alternative medicine, was writing a cookbook that he hoped to publish.

Then William was killed in an accident. My mother had just turned three. Her younger brother Gabriel (Gabe) was less than a year old, Carmela (Millie) was four, and Michael (Mike) was six. The night of the tragedy, my grandfather William had gone to work in the Hoboken railroad yard to cover for a friend who had a date with a girl. William—a true romantic and totally besotted with my grandmother, according to all sources—most likely wanted to give this man the same opportunity he had been given: to pursue the love of his life.

My grandfather's friend had the job of walking along the tops of the freight cars to make sure they were coupled before the train started moving. On this night, the train started taking off with my grandfather still atop one of the train cars, eyeballing the all-important coupler. He fell off and was crushed under the wheels. My mom can't remember many details of that terrible time. But one memory did endure.

My grandfather William had been gone three months when my grandmother Anna made the half-mile trek to her in-laws' home, carrying baby Gabriel while her three other small children walked alongside them. At this point, Anna had been suffering from rheumatoid arthritis for a few years, and walking was somewhat difficult. Anna and her children made their way up the steps of the large house and knocked on the door. The doorbell had been taken out of service, since William's mother— my great-grandmother Carmela—had awakened to the sound of it the night her son died. Carmela never wanted to hear the sound again.

Anna didn't view this excursion, her fourth in the last three months, as a last-ditch effort to make contact with her husband's parents. But her sister-in-law who answered the door felt otherwise.

"Anna, they're never going to see you," she said kindly. "Please, you need to stop coming here. I feel bad, but they're not going to change their minds."

Anna did as she was told and left that day never to return. My mother told me the story about the break between the families a few times, but my Grandma Anna never mentioned it. Since none of the parties involved are alive to defend themselves, the cause will remain a mystery.

In any case, my grandma Anna and her children lost a lot on that day. For all intents and purposes, they became an island unto themselves. My great-grandparents never saw Anna or any of the children again. Feeling cut off, the D'Annunzio children and Anna relied heavily upon her family, the Mastrangelos.

One Christmas day, when Mom was four and Millie was five, they were delighted to find two identical baby dolls under the Christmas tree. One for each of them, in a household where toys were always shared. Then one of those helpful Mastrangelo cousins came to call, and noticed Josephine and Millie each holding a brand-new baby doll. To my mother's shock, the cousin demanded one of the baby dolls for her own daughters to share.

"Millie and Josephine can share one doll," she reasoned.

My grandma Anna must have been caught off guard by her cousin's demand, and she had to make a couple of snap decisions. First, whether or not to give up a doll. Grandma must have figured that regular visits from a supportive member of her family were of more value than a plastic baby doll. Now, whose doll? Josephine was younger and tougher than Millie. Less likely to share her toys. Millie would be more likely to share her doll with Josephine. Josephine's doll had to be handed over. Grandma had to wrestle it out of Josephine's arms. It must have been a heart-wrenching scene. But perhaps Grandma figured someday Josephine would understand that this needed to be done for the good of the family, that it was nothing personal, and that she was not loved any less than Millie was. Perhaps Grandma figured someday Josephine would understand there was nothing she could have changed about herself to make her more deserving of that baby doll.

Grandma figured wrong.

The loss of the doll was an enduring source of sorrow for Mom, but the apartment house in Union City was a source of pride. The insurance payout from my grandfather's death on the railroad allowed my grandma Anna to purchase the six-family apartment building in Union City. To pay for food on the table and other necessities, Grandma Anna returned to work in New York City. Her profession was sewing sequins on dresses that would be sold in upscale department stores. My great-grand-mother Josephine helped raise the children. My great-grandfa-ther Michael grew grapes in the small backyard and drank his homemade wine and played cards with his buddies at all hours there. Having lost his fortune when a local bank failed during the Great Depression, he was a bitter man. My mother recalled him as complacent when not inebriated and frightful when he was. He was inebriated much of the time.

Fortunately, life in Union City in the 1930s also had its bright spots. My mother hated school but often pretended to be sick so she could attend daily Mass with her namesake, her sweet grandma Josephine. Mom recalls the orphans in front of the rectory at nearby St. Joseph's Church waving and calling out "Grandma" as they passed. Mom was always proud of how much her own mother and grandmother were loved by children in their neighborhood.

My grandma Anna would return home from work bone-tired and then deliver homemade pasta and lasagna to strug-gling families renting apartments from her. On a few occasions, she even washed lice out of the hair of their children. Of course my mother felt badly for the St. Joseph's orphans, and also for the children of the tenants who were somehow unable to pro-vide them with proper care. Then again, she and her three sib-lings had become accustomed to happiness tinged with sadness. They spent carefree days bicycling or roller skating or, when they were lucky, heading to nearby Palisades Amusement Park. But they always came home to an unpredictable and often surly grandfather.

"He could be nice, but not when he drank his homemade wine," my mother said. She was terrified of the man. The loving presence of her mother Anna and grandmother Josephine was a blessing. Frequent visits from Anna's only brother Lou and his wife Rosanna, along with their children, helped to soften the sting of loss. But I know that for my mother, at least, it wasn't enough.

In the late 1940s, Grandma Anna lost the apartment house due to non-payment of taxes. A woman with high standards but a soft heart, she had let too many residents slide on their rent payments. She lived with my aunt Millie and her family, first in Union City and then in Jackson, New Jersey. Her final years were spent in my parents' home, and then a nursing home. She never remarried, having lost the man she described as the love of her life.

I live with a fantasy in my head, a wishful interpretation of how things might have turned out had my grandfather not taken his friend's place atop the railroad cars on the fateful night. I can picture my grandparents living out their lives happily, retiring on a nice railroad pension. Maybe they would move to the country, where my grandfather would finish writing the vegetarian cookbook he started.

My mother and her siblings would have received the paternal love and guidance they needed. My grandfather, a bit of an independent thinker, would likely have allowed Uncle Mike to talk to the baseball scout who discovered him during his high school career. It was a conversation Grandma Anna forbade, fearing for her son's safety on the road.

Uncle Gabe might have received the help he needed to excel in his studies and not give up on school. Aunt Millie might have attended secretarial school. And my mother might have been given the violin and piano lessons she so desired. Perhaps the four of them would have had more rewarding careers and vocations.

Of course, it all sort of falls under the category of *Who knows?* But my existence hinges on another burning question. If he were alive, would my grandfather, who was a teetotaler like my mother and grandmother, have allowed Mom to marry my father, who was a beer drinker?

I have struggled with this question for years and have no clear answer. My mother loved my father deeply, and it would have been sad had that love been denied. On the other hand, between her grandfather and her husband, my mother had to deal with drinkers almost her entire life. It got old, I am sure.

So perhaps William D'Annunzio would have laid down the law and forced Joe Mandrick to choose between beer and his daughter.

And perhaps my father, desperately in love with my mother but more desperately needing a daily beer or two to numb the pain and guilt he still felt from his wartime experience, would have walked away.

But hopefully not.

Because my dad was indeed a good man.

Chapter Nineteen

Fiat Madness

BOTH OF MY PARENTS HAD A CHECKERED HISTORY WITH cars. This is especially true in my mother's case, even though she never had a driver's license.

It began when she was just a toddler, living on a street leading to Hudson Boulevard in Union City, New Jersey. My mom, little Josephine, managed to run out of the yard where she was being supervised by some older neighborhood kids after her bouncing ball ended up in the street. My asthmatic, widowed grandmother Anna was summoned out of her four-family home with cries of "A car just ran over Josephine!"

Grandma Anna ran out into the street to find that a car had indeed run over her daughter. Literally over. There was not a scratch on Josephine, who had had the presence of mind to do a spread-eagle onto the roadway and let the car pass right over her.

My mother's streak of "luck" continued a few years later, when my grandma Anna's brother Lou parked his car in front of the family's apartment house. The parked car was facing downhill toward nearby Hudson Boulevard, which was basically a busy four-lane highway with traffic lights. This was back in the day when grown-ups could relax in the house with a glass of wine and a plate of homemade pasta while the children played happily in the street.

Six-year-old Josephine made her way into the unlocked car and managed to engage the shift into gear. A bit farther down the hill was a man polishing his brand-new roadster in his driveway. Imagine his surprise when he saw an automobile approaching down the hill, quickly gaining speed and being driven by a little girl who could barely see over the steering wheel. My mother remembers the man doing a double-take at her uncle's car, then glancing toward the always-bustling boulevard directly downhill in the car's path.

Fortunately for little Josephine, this very startled man made a selfless split-second decision. He rolled his brand-new car into my mother's path, saving her from almost-certain death. My mother was once again unscathed, and my uncle's car was still drivable. The brand-new car was totaled. Wherever this man's descendants are, I hope they are rich and happy. I certainly hope *he* died at an old age—and rich and happy.

My badly shaken Uncle Lou never drove again. His wife Rosanna took the wheel, leading to other mishaps. Let's just say that if you saw my aunt's Cadillac sedan sailing down the street, you would be wise to step back from the curb. And the excitement didn't end there.

My mom always preferred things to be brand-new. My friends still describe her as "fancy." So when my dad promised to pick her up for their first date in a "nice" car, Mom told all her friends that she was being squired in a nice, *new* car. They gathered on the porch to get a glimpse of this shining new roadster, only to see a shining antiquity pull up to the house. Every time my mother told me this story and dramatically detailed her mortification at the sight of the classic but long-in-the-tooth car, my father would merely shrug his shoulders. The old versus new incident was merely a blip on the radar. Things were about to get worse for them, car-wise.

In the 1950s, my dad and his sister Bernice went mad for Fiat cars, an import from Italy. Dad had seen them zipping about during his Army tour of Italy. At that time he was eager for any distraction from his actual business of war. These included Italian wine, Italian girls, and Italian cars.

When I was born in 1958, my dad owned his first Fiat. It was an 1100 model and a beautiful shade of Wedgewood blue with nice rounded lines and a striking grille. In a world filled with orange and light green giant-finned American-made cars, the Fiats really stood out. They were stylish, extremely tiny, and overall a great conversation-starter.

On the downside, they were finicky about starting and they rusted like crazy. And as the joke went, Fiat actually stood for Fix It Again, Tony. Appropriately, my dad's mechanic was named Tony.

Shortly after I was born, the Fiat was once again in the shop with Tony, and Dad had to spend a few days hoofing it home from his evening shift at the Hostess cake factory. Luckily the two-mile walk was not a huge deal for my dad, who once rode a bicycle up and down the hills of the Palisades during his days as a messenger. He walked frequently, performed a lot of manual labor as a factory worker, and was still in tip-top shape.

One night, as he made his way across the viaduct leading from Hoboken to Union City, he was momentarily blinded by the headlights of a car. It took him a few seconds to realize the car was headed straight for him, and fortunately he had the agility to leap over the side of the viaduct and land on the pavement a few feet below. A policeman in a nearby patrol car witnessed the incident and assured my very shaken-up dad that it was most likely a case of mistaken identity. Of course, when he came home and told my mom about it, she blamed the Fiat.

The incident did not affect my dad's affection for the car in any way. Whether it was due to memories of sunny Italy or the fact that the car was a lot of fun to drive, he was totally smitten with his finicky Fiat. I can remember going with my dad to fetch my grandpa Joe on South Street in Jersey City for a ride to Keansburg. Keansburg was my dad's family's destination of choice, beginning with their childhood vacations through the times when they would return as adults.

In addition to the beachfront (on the Raritan Bay) and the fishing pier, the Keansburg amusement area of the early 1960s consisted of a tar-paved street lined with food, bars, rides, and games of chance. It was not a fancy place by any means, but for my dad and his father it was a bit of paradise rich with memories and shared solitude. I cherished the trips to Keansburg, with my tall and lanky grandpa folded into the front seat alongside my dad, bouncing merrily along. (I swear that the Fiats of that era had rubber bands for shocks.)

Grandpa Joe, who was amazingly broad-shouldered and stood six foot three, had to remove his trademark gray fedora in order to fit into the tiny Fiat. Sometimes my cousin Tom, my Aunt Gladys's son, would come along for the adventure. The two of us would enjoy rides and games while Dad and Grandpa Joe relaxed over beers at the Heidelberg restaurant.

The blue Fiat lasted through many adventures like this. The car lasted eleven years, which was pretty impressive. (Realistically, though, perhaps at least two years of that long shelf life was spent at Tony's garage. But never mind that.) Despite my mother's objections, we shopped for another Fiat upon the demise of the first.

My dad wanted to purchase the Fiat 850 Coupe, a sporty two-door with barely any room for back passengers. My mother pointed this out in the dealership, but my dad was too enthralled with the looks of the floor model to listen to her pleas. Sure, the four-door model 240 made a lot more sense. But the 850 Coupe came in a beautiful shade of hunter green with a dark tan interior! Dad and I were both dazzled, and the car was bought. As it turned out, my mother was right.

The Fiat 850 was neither reliable nor roomy. It received a lot of attention for its styling and, again, for its small size. So we did get the desired "Ah!" factor, even if it was sometimes "Ah! That car is so small! How do they fit in it?" I also grew dramatically in height from the time of the car's purchase until its eventual demise, so in order to fit into the back, I had to sit somewhat hunched over and with my head tilted forward. It is a posture that I have adopted to this day when I sit in the back of any car.

The Fiat 850, like its predecessor, did not like cold weather. It refused to start once the temperature dipped below forty degrees Fahrenheit. Fortunately, my father stumbled upon a solution. If he could get the car rolling downhill at a decent clip, he could somehow engage the engine using the stick shift. I don't know the mechanics of how this worked. I only know that we were fortunate to have a downward-sloping hill at the other end of our dead-end street.

If the Fiat felt that it was just too cold to venture out—and this usually happened in the middle of the night when my dad was due to start work on the night shift—my mother and I would be summoned to push the car to the other end of the block so Dad could turn left and go down the hill. I have to admit it was somewhat exciting to hear the starter engage the engine as Dad was halfway down the hill. Which, luckily, it did every time. Or else we would have had to push the car back *up* the hill.

Once Dad was on his way, he would give a triumphant wave, and Mom and I would make our way back to the house in our nightclothes under the forgiving cover of night. Or so we thought.

I have the unhappy recollection of one of the neighbor ladies informing me that she had seen my mother and me in our robes pushing the Fiat down the block and found it quite amusing. I am the type of person who usually has a smart answer for everything, but try as I might, I had absolutely no rejoinder for this particular remark.

Shortly after this, the car broke down just as my dad was ready to drive home from the Hostess factory in Hoboken (surprise), and my dad had to have it towed. The tow truck driver, unfamiliar with the standard shift mechanisms of foreign cars, neglected to make a needed adjustment. As a result, the Fiat was left without the ability to reverse. Mom and I were once again enlisted to back it into parallel parking spots, most often in the middle of the nearby Hackensack shopping district. At this point, we were pretty much immune to the stares of passersby.

My aunt Bernice's family has Fiat stories as well.

The Effingers were a two-car family, so not everyone had to pile into the Fiat. But when they did, the results were hilarious. My cousin Nancy remembers sitting in the back seat of the car and having to place her feet strategically so they did not hang down through the hole that had rusted through the floor of the car. She could literally see the road passing beneath her.

On one occasion Bernice's husband Paul made a sharp turn, and my cousin Bob slammed into the tinny passenger door, hitting the handle. The door promptly opened up. Luckily, Uncle Paul had the swift reaction of grabbing Bob by the collar before he spilled out onto the road. In my dad's family, every unfortunate incident was usually blamed on the person it happened *to*. I know that makes no sense, but it certainly put the fear of bad luck and stupidity into all of the Mandrick cousins. We became quite accustomed to the phrase "you dopey kids," which let us know, in no uncertain terms, that our ineptitude had somehow caused a bad situation. I can still remember my dad telling my mother the story and saying, "So Paul made a sharp turn and can you believe that dopey Bob *almost fell out of the car?*" I would have laughed, except for the chilling realization that this could happen at any time, to any one of us cousins.

After the 850 Coupe finally gave up the ghost, we were basically done with Fiats. My dad bought a four-door white Ford Maverick with power steering, an automatic transmission, and a fancy black double pinstripe painted down the side. But if you think the car drama was over, you are wrong. The Maverick was almost totaled a few weeks after my mother placed the statue of Saint Christopher, the patron saint of drivers, on the car's dashboard. Mom was very excited about the statue and our family's new American-made car. Not so much for my dad. Shortly afterward, he—the most cautious and careful driver on the planet—had his first car accident ever at the age of fifty-five.

The incident occurred at a nearby intersection with a traffic light, and there were no eyewitnesses. As a result, neither driver ended up being held accountable.

But you can guess who my dad considered to be at fault.

Chapter Twenty

There Goes My Hero

I ALMOST ALWAYS REMEMBER DETAILS OF MY DREAMS. IN a recurring dream that I have had since childhood—but one that went away after Dad's passing—Dad and I would be driving over a bridge in his tiny blue Fiat sedan. It was always the same bridge, a very tall and long one with sparkling white pavement, and the same car. Dad was always behind the wheel in this dream, steering in his careful and skillful way. Almost one hundred percent of the time, these dreams preceded a major event in my life. And they were reassuring. If there was anyone I always trusted to steer with absolute certainty, it was my dad. He was the safest driver on any road, perhaps due to his experience as an ambulance driver for injured soldiers during World War II.

My mom had been living with me for over a year when I realized that I hadn't had my usual dream, or any dream, about my father since he had passed away. I did have a dream about my dad a few days before he died, in which my aunt Bernice pulled up in her trusty but long-gone red Fiat and urged my father to get in, just like in the good old days. But in the dream, Dad walked right past me as if I wasn't there.

Being who I am, I saw the lack of attention from Dad in my dreams as an indictment of my past mistakes and my current care for my mom.

Shortly after, I added another request to my usual bedtime prayer repertoire.

"Please, God, I just need to see my father's face again," I said. "I need to know that he thinks I am doing the best I can for my mom."

A few nights later, I had a vivid dream about my dad.

In the dream, I was agitated and was standing in the street facing my parents' former home at Sixty-Eight Overlook Avenue in Ridgefield Park. In the driveway facing me was Dad's white Ford Maverick. We owned that car for a good ten years beginning in the 1970s, and Dad had taken great pride in keeping it clean and waxed.

In the dream I saw my dad—my *dad*—remove something from the trunk of the Maverick. In a second he was standing next to the driver's door of the car and facing me. I saw a snow scraper in his hand and realized this was my dad of the Maverick days. He was still over six feet tall and strongly built, with his almost-black hair just starting to gray at the temples. I took a breath, reminded of what a striking and even formidable figure he made at that age. Like his father before him, he was nonviolent. Yet somehow everyone knew not to mess with either Joe Sr. or Jr.

"I have to pick Mom up and get her to the train station by three," I yelled. I was willing him to hop into the car and offer to drive me to wherever Mom was. To take the wheel.

In the street, snow had fallen and was sparkling as though bits of diamond had fallen from the sky. Dad was nonplussed, as he always was in real life. Maybe even a little irritated. He disliked what he called scenes, and he despised yelling. He did not take a single step toward me.

"I know," he said as he began to wipe the snow ever so carefully off the car's front windshield. "I'm helping you," he continued in the same even voice, as though I really should have known this.

I woke up with a start. *I'm helping you.* I rolled those cherished words over and over in my head, reveling in the sound of them. I had forgotten what a doer my dad was, always working to pave the way for me and keep me safe.

Even though he reached a ripe old age, I still miss my dad every day. I miss him awful. I miss working to earn his tacit approval, and I miss knowing that he considered me capable of just about anything. I thought that, by allowing him to live to the age of ninety-five, God had given me enough of him to last my lifetime. I was wrong.

But my dream made it clear. It was time for me to grow up and stop seeking Dad's approval or expect him to keep me safe. It was time for me to take the wheel. As Dad would say almost jokingly when he could see me struggling, "Hop right in, the water's fine."

I no longer have any excuses for not doing just that. After all, Dad was thoughtful enough to clean the windshield for me.

Chapter Twenty-One

Show Me the Funny!

MY DAD WAS THE ONE JOHN CONNECTED WITH, DESPITE the fact that their relationship began on a rocky note. Mom had made her famous lasagna for John's first dinner at their home, which would have caused just about anyone else on the planet to drool with anticipation. But 1980s John was a notoriously fussy eater and had never eaten red sauce mixed with mozzarella and ricotta cheese. He later confided that he was quite nervous about not being able to enjoy the meal. If you ask him about it now, he laughs at the irony. He became the biggest fan of Mom's lasagna, quite literally.

Shortly after we sat down at the table, my dad decided to break the ice by telling John that he had a "nice Roman nose." I almost groaned. I knew where Dad was heading but felt helpless to stop him. And I also thought, No, he wouldn't dare.

John mumbled his thanks in a state of confusion and gave my dad the opening he was waiting for.

"Yeah, it's roamin' all over your face!" he said, and laughed at his own joke as he always did.

I caught John's eye, trying to send a silent "I'm sorry," and Mom rose from the table.

"Joe!" she yelled, which made my father laugh harder.

"I was just kidding," he said. "I'm sure John has a sense of humor."

Which was a challenge, I knew. "Laugh," I whispered while Dad was distracted by Mom's ire, and we both did.

Fast-forward thirty-four years. The week before he died, my father told my mother that he considered John his son, not his son-in-law. By that point, John had also become extremely close to my dad and affectionately referred to him as the "King of the One-Liners." He had a million of them.

My dad has always been funny on purpose, and even when his jokes or pranks fell flat, we had to laugh. Maybe because he himself would chuckle at the conclusion of his delivery, and it seemed downright rude not to join in. My father's conversation was always sprinkled with gems like these:

"They say married men live longer. Actually, it just seems that way."

"He has wavy hair. It is waving goodbye."

"You got a haircut? Why didn't you get them all cut?"

"I call my wife Crisco because she's fat in the can."

"I keep jumping for joy but I can never quite reach her."

"I went to a party and everyone was feeling rosy. Rosy got mad and went home."

"Stick around, we're opening a pot of glue."

"Her teeth are like the stars, they always come out at night."

"Did you hear about the fire at the shoe factory? Ten thousand soles were lost."

Veronica always enjoyed this one:

"It's a good day for the race!"

"Which race is that, Grampy?"

"The human race!"

But wait, there are more . . .

John came up with the name "Queen of the Malapropisms" for my mother. He also calls her Slip Mahoney, in memory of a character from the Bowery Boys movies who always mangled the English language.

My mother gamely managed a reaction to my dad's jokes even after the hundredth telling (usually a smirk or an eye roll, but a good-natured one). Not only that, but she is funny in her own right. And almost always it's not on purpose. Which makes her even funnier, let's face it:

"We just saw that movie, *Terms of Endurement*."

"She is in her period of moaning" (she meant mourning).

"You need to get Greg some flammable pajamas." (This was left on my answering machine when my son was five years old. She meant flannel. Not inflammable. Flannel.)

"Your stomachache will go away if you take some Pepto Dismal!"

"I don't want to eat too much and gouge myself."

"We need some alumimum ferl."

"*Free Wooly* is a nice movie for the kids."

"Steinfeld is on."

My dad worked on the assembly line at Hostess cake for many years, rustling pans and packaging those perfect little cupcakes with the white swirl down the middle. He was well-respected and well-liked by his longtime foreman, who offered him a promotion to baker. This was a big deal. And my father turned it down. I was unaware that this happened, but my mother told me about it years later. His reasoning at the time was that the bakers worked with a lot of flour, but they did not wear masks to protect their lungs. They were not required and not provided. When my dad brought this point up to his fore-man, he was ridiculed and rebuffed. Realizing he was in danger of being considered a troublemaker and thereby losing his good standing, my dad rejected the offer.

"Those men are all dead now from lung cancer," my mother told me years later as my dad sat peacefully in his armchair and nodded.

"What a shame," he said.

A few years after turning down the promotion, my father was there to save those same bakers from impending doom. They had gotten locked in the walk-in oven, unable to push the door open from the inside. Hearing their frantic knocks and cries, and realizing the dire situation, everyone else on the factory floor froze. My dad was the only one with the presence of mind to open the door, step in, and get them safely out.

Sometimes not being what society deems as "successful" ends up placing you in the right place at the right time. My dad was a hero that day.

He ended up being a role model and sort of a hero to John as well, especially after John lost his own dad to cancer in 2000. My dad was around for John until 2013. And although John welcomed Mom into our home with open arms a year later, I can't help but feel part of him wished it were Dad instead. They shared an enjoyment of old movies, model trains, long walks, and afternoons spent sitting on our patio in companionable silence. And, like Dad, John came to enjoy trips to Atlantic City.

One day when Mom was living with us, I saw a look of sadness on John's face. It wasn't the first time. Between Mom and me, John was dealing with a lot. But this time I sensed that John was missing Dad. Before Mom woke up, we'd spent the morning talking about the good old days in Atlantic City, when my aunt Betty would join us and Mom would pile gastronomically incompatible foods from the buffet onto Dad's plate. Dad would refuse to eat what Mom had glopped together, and John would fetch him the plate of shrimp he wanted in the first place. Mom would get aggravated and try to eat what she had gotten for Dad. "Oh, this is a terrible combination," she would say, as though someone else were responsible.

"Are you thinking about Dad?" I asked. John said he was, and I had an idea. When I was a child, my dad sometimes took Mom and me on "mystery drives." Sometimes they ended at a place she enjoyed, such as Van Saun Park in nearby Paramus. I never thought of my mom as a nature lover, but she just loved to feed the ducks there. Once in a while, the mystery drive would end at Palisades Amusement Park in nearby Fort Lee, where I could enjoy all of the rides and attractions. I decided to treat John and Mom to a mystery ride.

Neither of them seemed thrilled as we placed Mom carefully in the car. "I have a feeling I know where we're headed, and I think you're crazy," John said after we had spent a half hour traveling south on the Garden State Parkway.

"I know I'm crazy," I said. "And it's going to be fine." Mom offered no opinion, since she was fast asleep next to me in the front passenger seat.

I decided on the Borgata casino, and Mom laughed as I wheeled her in. "Oh, this is a surprise," she said. "It's too bad I don't like Atlantic City." I did know that going in. But I wanted this day to be about John. "You will like the buffet, though," I said. Luckily, she did. I had brought some money for gambling, and I sat next to Mom and helped her operate a slot machine. We were holding even by the time John rejoined us an hour later.

"I'll stay with Mom while you play a machine," John offered.

He didn't have to ask twice. I spent a relaxing half hour watching the reels spin on one of my favorite slot machines before suddenly feeling compelled to check on John and Mom. I was glad I did, because John looked unusually wild-eyed. Mom, meanwhile, was squinting at the screen of a "Match Game" slot machine, based on the popular television show. As I walked over, I saw John taking Mom's money out of the machine.

"She's winning, but we have to leave right now," John explained.

"Why?" I asked.

"I'll tell you later," he said, and we quickly made our way to the car. My mom, exhausted by all of the activity, fell asleep just minutes into the ride home.

"So, what happened?" I asked John when I realized Mom was out cold and wouldn't hear our conversation.

"Well, Mom and I were playing the machine, and we had to pick the winning answers like contestants do on the show," John explained. "She couldn't really see very well, so she just kept picking the third answer on the screen. And she was winning. But then she asked what the answer was, the one she won on, and I couldn't tell her. So we had to leave."

"Why, what was the answer?" I asked. I knew the TV game show could get sort of salty, but I did not expect that the slot machine game would. Apparently, I was wrong. John's face turned red.

"The answer was 'boobies'!" he said. I laughed.

"Boobies?" I said.

"Boobies!" he repeated.

"We had to leave because of boobies?" I said. I hated leaving Atlantic City more than I hated leaving Palisades Amusement Park. I didn't know which was more ridiculous, the fact that we had brought Mom to Atlantic City in the first place, or the reason why we'd left. It was all sort of funny, and I thought about how the King of the One-Liners might have actually been proud of us for daring to be ridiculous.

John knew he was being put on the defensive, and he got angry. "Yes, because of boobies!" he yelled.

I had to smile. John could never lie to my mom, making up another word to tell her. And he certainly could never say the word "boobies" to her. He was unfailingly honest and respectful. And here I was, doubting him.

I was about to apologize when I heard Mom's voice.

"Did John just say 'boobies'?" she asked from the passenger seat. I laughed as John's face turned from red to ghostly white, and he gripped the steering wheel more tightly. I couldn't lie to my mom, either. But this wasn't a problem. With Mom's short-term memory pretty much gone, she wouldn't remember. Dementia takes away, but on that day it gave me the freedom to be honest without worry of repercussion. So I told Mom the truth. The whole truth. To her credit, she laughed heartily.

"Oh, poor John," she said as the color returned to John's face. The things we put that poor man through, I said to myself. "So, I won?" Mom asked before closing her eyes again.

"You won forty dollars!" John answered loudly. I could hear the relief in his voice.

"Oh boy, that's good," she said. "Spend it on yourself, John. I insist." John and I exchanged a look. Whenever my dad won a slot machine jackpot of more than two hundred dollars, which happened during almost every trip to Atlantic City, he would offer some gambling money to John and me. "Oh no, you keep it, Dad," we would say. "No," he would answer, pushing the cash toward us. "I insist."

Sure, it might have been sheer madness to think that a last-minute trip to Atlantic City with my elderly mom in tow would be a good idea, but somehow it worked. Now we had forty extra bucks, and Mom had enjoyed a great buffet meal and some laughs at John's expense. John, for his part, looked happier than he had in a long while.

"Take Mom's winnings and whatever we have left from today and spend it on yourself," John said.

"Are you sure?" I asked.

"I insist!" he answered.

Chapter Twenty-Two

The Josephine Zone

MY NEIGHBOR DEBBIE DID US A HUGE FAVOR ONE COLD winter's day. Our free-of-charge granny-sitters, Greg and Veronica, had returned to their respective schools after winter break. We'd spent money on Christmas gifts, more than usual. We were under financial strain and experiencing a case of cabin fever as well. When Debbie stopped by on a Saturday morning and offered to wake Mom after her afternoon nap and share dinner in front of the TV set, we hesitated. When she insisted, we were thrilled.

John and I were well aware that when we moved Mom in, we would be giving up some of our autonomy and privacy. But I wasn't quite prepared for how much of my freedom I would lose, and how it would impact the "fun" aspect that had been such an important part of our marriage. It felt like Mom and I had somehow become more of a couple than John and I. We thanked Debbie profusely upon our return home from an inexpensive dinner out.

"Oh, it was not a problem, really," she said. "I miss caring for my own mom, and your mother is such a sweetheart. Life is good in the Josephine Zone."

When Debbie mentioned the Josephine Zone, I had to laugh. She made a good point. I always recall my family's small bungalow in Ridgefield Park as a safe haven, and I felt the same way about my parents' apartment in Long Branch. I mistakenly assumed it was because both places were in beautiful locations and were kept immaculately clean by Mom. But then I gave serious thought to what Debbie said and came to this conclusion:

The Josephine Zone has nothing to do with where Mom is at the moment and everything to do with her mindset.

I have always known that my mother was a powerful force, and I used to refer to her as a "force of nature." Now I know that the source of her power goes much deeper than that. Like everyone else, she has dreams that were never realized. A trip to Hawaii. A bigger house near a park where she could see people interact and watch children play. Money to spend on her grandkids to provide them with gifts or to just help them out when they need it.

But, like her sister Millie, who endured the same childhood tragedies and similar grown-up disappointments, my mother perseveres. She wakes up every morning knowing that she is blessed to have another day on earth. Especially if that day begins with a cup of coffee. (Of course, if that coffee doesn't have the right amount of sugar and milk thoroughly mixed in, there will be hell to pay.)

At some point when I was growing up, my mother's reputation for being nonjudgmental and delivering sound advice became a known quantity not only in our family, but throughout our town. In a scene reminiscent of the *The Godfather*, people my mother knew, sometimes only marginally, actually showed up at our door unannounced seeking her "favor," in the form of guidance. I often listened in from my first-floor bedroom in our tiny home as they shared their troubles. There were hushed stories of teenagers having sex and drinking or even addicted to drugs, husbands cheating on wives, financial struggles that would surely lead to the loss of the family home. I don't know whether I was more fascinated by their stories or by my mother's sound advice.

Due to her strict Catholic upbringing, my mother saw things as right or wrong and black or white. There was no gray area. But here she was delving into the gray area and emerging unscathed. People didn't always leave with the answers they wanted to hear, but they left feeling better about themselves and their situations. They left feeling validated.

One person my mother helped was her good friend Carmen. I don't recall how my mother and Carmen met—perhaps they worked at the same factory. (Mom held a series of short-running assembly line jobs until finding her niche at the nearby Fabergé factory.) Perhaps they knew each other from the playground, since Carmen lived a few blocks away and her son was in my grade at school.

The point is that Carmen became very dependent on Mom. She phoned Mom on a daily basis from the time I entered high school until she and her husband moved away in 1983. That's eleven years. Sometimes the phone calls were brief. Sometimes they could drag on for an hour or more. Carmen's troubles were, as my father would say, nothing to sneeze at. A philandering husband. A son who was being bullied. Another son who was abusing drugs. And then, finally, the last straw. Carmen's husband ordered a brain scan to try to get at the heart of her depressive episodes. And Carmen was convinced that the resulting exposure to radiation caused an increase in her depressive episodes and made her sick. That's when the phone began to ring at least twice a day.

Of course, Mom had no solution to Carmen's problems, or at least none that Carmen was willing to take. But Mom was willing to listen, even as her afternoon cup of coffee got cold or dinner was delayed. To Dad's and my dismay, Mom didn't seem overly concerned about cold dinners. She was on a mission to help her friend.

In the spring of 1983, I was in my own head, planning my upcoming wedding. Mom was helping me out with the seating chart when the phone on her kitchen wall rang and Mom asked me to answer it because she was making us coffee. It was Carmen calling, and I hoped she could keep the conversation brief. I had minimal interest in Carmen and her troubles. I felt that time to plan my wedding was a-wastin'. For years I had resented the time Mom spent on the phone with Carmen.

"I'll get my mom," I said impatiently.

"Wait a second, sweetie," Carmen said in her gravelly chain-smoker's voice. "I need to tell you something."

I didn't respond. I took a step toward Mom, who was across the room.

"Your mother is a good woman," Carmen said. "She never gave up on anyone, not even me."

I took another step toward Mom.

"Don't ever forget that," Carmen said into the air, as I was already holding the phone away from my ear.

"I'll get her," I replied distractedly, stretching the phone cord as I handed the receiver to my mom with a scowl.

Chapter Twenty-Three

Babe

"OH," MOM SAID AS I LIFTED HER OFF THE BATHING BENCH.

"What?" I said. I was getting tired of the "ouches" and "ohs" associated with the small discomforts Mom endured when I bathed her.

Although Mom despised them, I knew baths at least once a week were a must. I performed this task grudgingly, resenting the fact that my kids were gone and my house was now filled with aging creatures who sometimes didn't smell so good.

Sadly, I was one of them.

On my good days, I was able to put myself in Mom's shoes and understand she missed having control over things like bath water temperature. She had always showered daily, as soon as she woke up. Now she had to rely on my help, and I'm sure she was frustrated. "I hate the bath," she would say during the trip from her bedroom as she gripped the hallway handrails and stumbled like a drunken sailor. On good days, I would laugh and Mom would, too. But this was not a good day.

"You know I'm not hurting you!" I said.

"Oh, I don't know why I am so sensitive," she said, clearly embarrassed. "And at my age."

I suppressed a sigh.

Mom continued talking as I helped her out of the tub. "You know, my family used to make fun of me for being sensitive," she said. "They used to call me something, but I forget what it was."

"Babe," I answered, although I didn't want to. Mom was beautiful as a young girl, but that was not the reason for the nickname. "Babe" was short for "Baby." Mom was a fearful young child, often clinging to the adults in her life. Her older sister Millie was outgoing and adventurous. Josephine had to be convinced to leave the house on most days.

I remained silent, and Mom spoke again after furrowing her brow. "I'm not sure why, but now I feel bad; but that's silly, isn't it?"

I shrugged noncommittally. I wanted to get the bath over with, although I didn't have anything else compelling to accomplish. I was just being impatient.

"Feeling bad doesn't change anything, does it?"

And I had to smile. As usual, she was right. I regretted my surly mood and apologized to Mom. Her eyes looked blank, as if she were confused, but she nodded. I wasn't sure, with her short-term memory gone, if she even remembered that I'd been impatient with her moments before. But I did. And I guess that's what counts.

One day years before, when Mom was living in the Long Branch apartment with Dad, she had asked me a favor. Could I possibly pick her up some of her favorite perfume? It was a simple request. And yet, selfishly, I couldn't bring myself to do it. It was as though every resentment I'd harbored against her and my dad had settled inside my head. I felt bad about my inaction but couldn't find my way around it. My cousin Barbara, who was ever solicitous to her mom, my aunt Millie, asked me a few weeks later if I had bought the perfume yet. At first I was rankled, and then I realized how wrong my stance was. Why was I torturing myself and my mom by reliving unpleasant moments and disappointments? I decided to focus on the things my parents had done right, and there were plenty. It was then I was able to head into the department store to make my purchase and deliver it to my grateful mom.

My friend shared a theory with me years ago that you choose your parents based on what you most desire in life. If that is true, I certainly chose parents who cherished me and kept me safe. For a long while, I wished for parents who would give me things—vacations, nice clothes, college tuition, or a wedding. I used to believe that safety was boring. I wanted more freedom and more fun. Then I finally grew up.

When I was a young girl, Mom used to dazzle me with stories about a troupe of trapeze artists called the Flying Wallendas. Mom explained that members of the troupe performed high wire acts without a safety net, resulting in a few fatalities over the years. Mom was horrified by this behavior. Why would you ever want to perform without a safety net? Even worse, why would you continue to do so after it had proved deadly to other members of your troupe? As I got older, I wondered about my mom's fascination with the Flying Wallendas. I thought perhaps she was intrigued by the recklessness of it all. I now realize that, without a father figure in her life and with a mother who was working most of the time, Mom spent her growing-up years feeling she didn't have a safety net. Caution, shyness, good sense, and good luck kept her from serious harm. She'd somehow managed to survive. But she never really got to perform the feats she might have been capable of.

When I handed Mom the perfume years ago, I saw much gratitude in her eyes. I also saw something else.

I saw my safety net.

One day, after giving Mom a bath and preparing her for an afternoon nap, I burst into tears.

"What's wrong?" Mom asked. She didn't seem alarmed, and I wasn't surprised. Mom had a history of overreacting to the little things in life but maintaining an amazingly calm exterior throughout life's bigger calamities. And with this serenity came wisdom. This pattern was still holding, even with the dementia. I could see Mom's wheels spinning, and I decided to tell her the truth. I really did need her guidance and reassurance.

"I'm worried about Veronica," I confessed. My daughter had been diagnosed with Lyme disease during her second semester of college, at age eighteen. I too had suffered from this insidious disease, enduring physical and mental agony. I had been diagnosed around the time my parents moved to Long Branch and had taken antibiotics for three years. Lyme had sapped my energy and my spirit, caused my entire body to ache after any physical activity, and made me think I might be going mad. Added to all this were the side effects of the antibiotics and supplements prescribed. I eventually recovered, but it took four years. Could my daughter do the same? She seemed to have a tougher case, with a co-infection of babesiosa—a malaria-like illness that is even tougher to treat than Lyme. Even worse, she'd had the disease for one to four years, according to the results of the blood test. I'd had Veronica tested for Lyme, but through more traditional labs. She'd tested negative twice, and I was relieved. But when her symptoms persisted, I finally brought her to the same Lyme-literate doctor who had saved me. Veronica was stoic and level-headed when diagnosed. Although she was tempted to take off a semester from college, she didn't. I was in awe of her determination and bravery. Still, my sadness over her suffering and my guilt over her late-term diagnosis permeated every second of every day for me at that difficult time.

"Why are you worried about Veronica?" Mom asked, eyebrows raised.

"I'm afraid she'll never get over the Lyme disease," I said. "I'm afraid she's always going to be sick."

"Now, you listen to me," Mom said, sitting on the bed and pointing a crooked, arthritis-ridden finger firmly in my direction. "Veronica is going to be okay. I feel it in my bones. And when I feel something in my bones, it always happens. It's going to take a little time. But she is young, and she is strong, and she will be cured. She will get better. That's the way it is. That's the way God wants it."

I felt such relief, I cried harder. When I had calmed down, I thanked my mom and tucked her in and kissed her forehead. As I did so, I thought about Carmen, Mom's friend from years ago, and her real and imagined illnesses. For years I had worried about money and material things, including my wardrobe and appearance. I hadn't worried overly much about my health until Lyme struck. But here I was, faced with an agonizing situation caused by an insect the size of a pinhead that had happened to latch onto my daughter. And here was my mom, faced with mental health problems of her own and yet able to lift me up and reassure me in a way no one else possibly could.

I never knew how much grief and stress an illness could cause. Before I left my mom's room, I said a silent prayer of thanks for my mom and her wisdom. And I mouthed a silent "I'm sorry" to Carmen, whose troubles I had minimized all those years ago.

Chapter Twenty-Four

Ginger Rogers

"GIVE ME A MINUTE," I TOLD MY MOTHER AT LEAST TEN times a day in response to her many questions.

"What am I doing with this water, am I drinking it?"

"I think I dropped a pill and can't find it."

"Am I going to bed now or watching TV?"

"Am I eating the rest of this food?"

"Am I drinking the rest of this coffee?"

"What am I supposed to be doing now?"

My mother was consistently confused about her routine, and I was overwhelmed. "Give me a minute" was what I learned to say. It gave me time to think and to breathe, or to walk away and ask myself how much longer I could do this.

"Give me a minute, give me a minute." I was tired of hearing myself say it. Mom would be sick of it for sure, but she couldn't remember much from one minute to the next. She had no idea how often I bought myself time with these words.

"Okay," she always answered. Mostly sweetly, sometimes warily, and sometimes gruffly. Even people with dementia are allowed to have mood swings. Thank God, because it is sometimes the only reminder that my mother is still my mother.

When Mom was living with me and I was her caregiver, I wondered what it was like for her to be on the other end of things. I know, because she said so, that she felt guilty. "You poor thing," was how she phrased it. In truth, the "poor thing" was Mom. She cared for Dad in their small apartment by the ocean for eleven years. His questions were endless, yet she rarely lost her patience. And even when she did, her mild irritation was always tinged with love and humor. Dad could have been a great stand-up comic, with his rapid-fire delivery:

"Where are my glasses?"

"Can you get me a beer?"

"Make your daughter a cup of tea."

"Get out the cookies."

"When can we go to Atlantic City again?"

"Wait a minute," my mother almost always answered, sounding exasperated.

"'*Wait* a minute,' what do you mean, 'wait a minute'?" my father would answer. "What are we waiting for, pray tell? A train or a bus, dear?"

He pretended to be kidding, shooting me a wink and a smile, but there was an archness to his voice that told me he was not pleased. Still I would always laugh a little when my dad winked. He would laugh, too, and my mother would put her hand on her forehead.

"*Aspetta, aspetta*," she would say quietly so my somewhat deaf father would not hear. The word for "wait" was about the only one she could recall in the native language of her Italian grandmother, and just saying it seemed to calm her down.

My dad was as sharp as a tack until the end of his days. Which should have made things easier, I suppose, but it didn't. He could be a handful. And most of mom's heavy lifting occurred when she was in her eighties. If I was Fred Astaire, somewhat highly regarded for my grace under pressure, she was Ginger Rogers— dancing backward in high heels. Doing everything I was, and doing it the hard way.

One afternoon about eight years ago, when Dad was ninety and Mom was eighty, I dropped her off at the local Foodtown in Long Branch to do some food shopping. Yes, God bless her, she was still capable of this at the age of eighty. We had just finished up with Dad's heart doctor appointment, and I was looking to kill time by driving him around while Mom shopped. Dad wanted me to buy some instant lottery tickets for John and me on his dime. Dad was always waiting for a big payday, whether in Atlantic City or by playing the lottery.

We were heading back to the Foodtown when Dad suddenly went totally rigid. He leaned back in the seat, his eyes wide and uncomprehending. I was at a loss for what to do.

"Dad, Dad!" I screamed as I pulled the car to the curb. He was still looking in the same direction, eyes wide and hands clenched, as I yelled again. "Daddy! Daddy! Wake up!"

I had just decided to turn the car around and head in the opposite direction to the emergency room of nearby Monmouth Medical Center when Dad suddenly came to.

"Dad, oh Dad, thank God!" I screamed, and his face went from startled to angry.

"Why were you yelling at me?" he said.

"Daddy, I thought you were dead!" I answered.

"Well, I wasn't, and you were yelling," he said. He was still sore at me.

"I think I should take you to the hospital," I said. Dad hated hospitals.

"You were yelling at me for no reason and now you think *I* need to go to the hospital?" he groused. "Let's get your mother."

I was feeling very foolish. Not about yelling, necessarily, but about the fact that any sane person would be heading to the hospital. Yet I still drove to the Foodtown. My father rarely got really angry, and when he did you were best advised to not rock the boat. I left Dad in the car, looking back to make sure he was not having yet another episode, and ran into the Foodtown to get my mom. I was sure that she would be very upset with me for not taking Dad to the hospital. I found her in the laundry detergent aisle.

"Mom," I yelled, tears filling my eyes. "Something just happened with Dad!"

I told her the story.

She listened, then furrowed her brow. "So he's all right now?"

"Well, yes, but…" I faltered. I was shocked at her composure. Or was it a total lack of concern? Perhaps she knew, as I did, that taking Dad to the hospital would result in an endless harangue later on. Maybe she could picture it—Dad being checked out in the hospital and given the all clear, only to return home later that night and make her feel guilty for "putting Mary Ann out."

"Poor Mary Ann had to take you food shopping and take me to the hospital besides, and you made her do it? Jeez," he would say as she silently prayed to one of her many favorite saints.

Mom convinced me it was best if she finished her food shopping and we all just went back to the apartment like nothing happened. After all, he seemed fine now. Right?

And so we did. Mom shopped purposefully, at her usual pace, which my dad would describe as molasses running uphill. I was busy sniffling and stressing and sort of carrying on.

At one point I stepped away to call Dad's doctor's office. The receptionist, who had known my parents and me for years, asked for the details of the episode and let me off the hook.

"He'll be in for a checkup in a few days; don't worry about it," she said.

Mom wanted my help with shopping, but I was still feeling the aftereffects of the past half hour. I had been convinced my dad was gone. And then, in an instant, he was back. It was unnerving, to say the least.

"Can you help me find the chicken soup Daddy likes, with the skinny noodles?" she asked.

I became lightheaded as I turned to help her. I gripped the handle of the shopping cart to regain my balance and focus.

"Give me a minute," is what I remember saying.

Chapter Twenty-Five

The Second Time Around

IF THE PROCESS OF CARING FOR MY MOM WASN'T THE going-down-in-flames debacle it could have been, I have my past experience to thank. In other words, it wasn't my first time at the rodeo.

My grandma Anna moved in with us when I was just beginning high school. I was beyond excited. I adored my grandma, even though she never tired of telling me that I was too skinny.

The biggest issue was how to fit her into our little house. We had five rooms, including two bedrooms. The answer was to give Grandma my bedroom and arrange for me to sleep on a borrowed cot-style bed in the living room. So Grandma became the purple princess in my lavender kingdom and slept on my prized gold-trimmed twin bed from Sears. My grandmother was all of four feet and eight inches tall, with creamy white hair and sparkling brown eyes. The whole setup suited her.

Me, not so much. Cramming my five-foot-seven self onto that cot and trying to get a full night's sleep was a challenge. And while Grandma Anna was a very pleasant woman, my father always had a huge need for quiet and privacy. With three women in the house often chatting or making remarks during television shows, his patience was worn thin. My mother was not herself, either, and became more critical of my behavior and appearance. It was a tough time for all of us, as my parents realized they might have bitten off more than they could chew.

Somehow it was all worth it. My grandmother had always been a loving presence and guiding force, and the sound of her frequent laughter in our house was music to my ears. Some of the best times of my life occurred when my father's sister Bernice came to visit, and everyone sat in the kitchen telling stories and just feeling loved. Like everyone else, Aunt Bernice enjoyed my grandmother's company immensely. Having two of my favorite people in our cheery yellow kitchen and sharing "coffee talk" with them was a wonderful experience.

Two years after Grandma moved in, it became apparent that along with her limited mobility (due to arthritis) came some mental challenges. She began yelling out in her sleep at night, frightening me and infuriating my dad. Her diabetes worsened, resulting in failing health. As time went on, the tension between my parents became so high that I feared that they might split up.

"Are you getting a divorce?" I once asked my parents.

"We can't afford one," they answered in unison. How reassuring.

After a few years, Grandma ended up in the hospital and was sent directly to a nursing home. I recall my mother's tearful days during that time, and her sadness and self-blame. To her credit, my mother had up to that point kept her full-time factory job and basically run a nursing home—albeit for a single resident—at the same time. This came with an unfortunate side effect, a disconnect on her part when I needed her most. And even though I was able to reclaim my mother and my bedroom, I missed my grandma terribly when she left.

To this day I sometimes decompress by recalling the peace and contentment of sitting with her in our small living room and enjoying *The Mike Douglas Show* and the lineup of afternoon mysteries and detective shows. (Often my mother would arrive home from work just in time for *McMillan & Wife* with Rock Hudson and Susan Saint James, and she would say that if she had Susan Saint James' body, she would wear just a T-shirt to bed as well—every single time. And my ultra-conservative grandma would pretend not to hear.)

My mother often brings up the fact that I helped out with Grandma Anna, but in truth she gives me way too much credit. She was the one doing the work, emotionally and physically. Just as I am now.

In retrospect, Grandma ended up giving us a lot more than we gave her in terms of unconditional love, kindness, and sheer joy. I enjoyed taking care of my grandma. As I recall, I had endless stores of patience for her.

You want another sandwich? No problem. Change the channel? Sure. A cup of coffee? Coming right up. Sit and chat with you instead of running out the door so much? That's fine, too.

I tried to be as patient with my mom, but some days were tougher than others. My patience was limited, and I lacked the "we can do this" attitude that I enjoyed when I was a teenager dealing with Grandma.

What happened? First and foremost, I had gotten much older. But it was more than that.

The added stressor was fear. When I looked at Grandma, I did not see my future. When I looked at my mom, I did. It unnerved me.

I confessed this to a group of friends while Mom was living with me. "My fear is that I will get dementia like my mother, but I won't be as adorable and pleasant as she is," I said.

No one answered for a few seconds, and then my fearless friend Paul spoke up. "First of all, you could *never* be as adorable as your mom is," he said, adopting a menacing pose and nasty expression. "You're gonna be a cranky old lady yelling 'Hey, you kids get off my lawn!'"

Never one to let a chance for additional comic relief pass me by, I responded to Paul's statement. "Except I'll be confused and yelling at my own grandkids," I pointed out.

We all laughed. It was a relief to put one of my biggest fears out there and end up being teased by my funny friend. But the fear about dementia being in my future gave me serious pause. I was not myself that night. I usually love the celebration of New Year's Eve. My neighbors throw terrific parties, and I always spend the evening with friends who are upbeat and hopeful about the future.

I had been somewhat optimistic at the beginning of 2016. I had even created a "2016 Wish List" poster with encouragement from my Zumba dance instructor, Evelyn. Evening sessions with Evelyn in nearby Long Branch were the highlight of my week. I was pleased to be invited to the poster-making event and to enjoy a non-Zumba activity with my classmates. We chatted as we clipped photos and lettering out of an assortment of magazines and glued them onto our Wish List posters. Mine included travel to the Bahamas and to Europe, and the titles of a few Broadway plays, along with the more realistic goal of new houseplants. The group enjoyed a laugh when I explained the inclusion of house plants on my poster. We all knew these posters was supposed to be the stuff of fantasy. Yet I had thrown a very realistic goal onto mine. I knew that out of everyone in the group, I had the smallest shot of achieving any fantasy goals. Yet I still harbored some hope. Now here I was at the end of 2016, and I had indeed only upgraded a few of my house plants.

As we toasted the New Year of 2017 later that night, I had no thoughts of "better days ahead." I was just hoping that Mom—who was sleeping soundly in her bed two houses away—would get through the year without any major mishaps.

I was trying not to be a damper on my friends' and John's high spirits. Yet I felt myself sinking to a low point. I used to wonder how I could possibly have episodes of depression, since I consider myself an optimist.

And then it dawned on me. You don't have to be a pessimist to be depressed. You can also be a disappointed optimist.

Chapter Twenty-Six

Diner

MY MANDRICK RELATIVES, UPON FIRST MEETING SOME-
one, would train their laser-focus eyes into that person's soul
and decide then and there whether that person was worth their
while.

My D'Annunzio relatives would hug you first and ask questions later.

Despite this obvious difference, I love both sides of my family equally. I especially adore my cousins, and I am blessed with
many of them.

One of the reasons why we moved "down the shore" was to
be closer to my aunt Millie's children, my cousins Joe, Barbara,
and Lois.

The four of us have happy memories of our halcyon days in
Union City, as well as an enduring adoration of our grandma
Anna. Like our beloved grandma, Barbara and Lois and Joe
have always represented a soft landing for me. Being with them
feels like coming home.

Like me, my three cousins cared for their widowed mother. It
was not a perfect science, but we really did try our best.

As my cousin Barbara said, "We have good days and bad days,
the four of us, but we can always count on the fact that we will
get one another through this." She should know. My aunt lived
with Barbara for years until she passed away in December 2017.

Barbara is a lot like my mother used to be. She always has a million things going on. "Lots of irons in the fire," as my father would say. Yet her hectic life somehow makes her even more solid and strong. If there has ever been a harsh word between us, or between Lois or Joe and me, I can't recall it.

But on this particular afternoon, I feared this wonderful track record of nonstop civility might be broken.

My cousins Barbara and Lois looked careworn. Shamefully, I was partly to blame.

The plan was for Barbara to bring Aunt Millie to a local diner, where Lois and Mom and I would meet them for lunch. Lois drove separately, as did Mom and I.

First, Lois and Barbara had a miscommunication about where they would meet to get Aunt Millie's hair trimmed and styled. This resulted in some aimless wandering on Lois's part and added stress for Barbara, who felt guilty about misdirecting Lois. I had added to the cray-cray by managing to misread a text from Barbara and arriving at the diner in a tizzy thinking they were already there. (They weren't.) I then texted both of them and managed to confuse them both even further.

This initial confusion took a toll on our moods and energy levels. Lois appeared tired, Barbara was pale, and I was wearing no makeup and had not styled my hair at all. I had also managed to button my jean jacket the wrong way in my hurry to leave the house.

Unlike us, my mother and her sister Millie were chic and smart and unruffled. My aunt's freshly shorn snow-white hair was gleaming, and she flashed her brilliant smile as she greeted my mother with a peck on the cheek shortly after we were seated at a round table. My mother—although in a state of confusion and not nearly as on as I had hoped she would be—grasped her sister's slim shoulder warmly after a moment of initial surprise.

"How are you doing, Millie?" she asked.

Unlike most people, Aunt Millie never worried about my mother no longer recognizing her. I used to question my aunt's confidence until it dawned on me that my aunt just knew the truth. She was the last person on earth my mother would ever forget. I'm including myself in that reckoning. Their sisterly bond was unrivaled, and their visits often ended with Aunt Millie singing her self-composed "sisters" song. "Sister, sister, I love my sister," is the repeated line.

"I'm great, Jo, how about you?" Aunt Millie answered.

"I'm good. Mary Ann and John do everything for me. . . . I don't worry about a thing," she said, and shrugged her shoulders.

I sat there wishing that "great" and "good" were words that could be used to describe my cousins and me. I was doing my best to get somewhat chill and falling short. My cousins still looked frazzled. I half wished the server could bring the three of us three sedatives along with the requisite glasses of water.

"Do they serve booze here?" my cousins asked one another as I began to perspire with the familiar beginnings of a hot flash.

"What did they say?" my aunt and mother asked me, and I felt beads of water pop out on my forehead.

They need a stiff one, I almost said, and bit my tongue. Although they are staunch Catholics and self-confessed prudes (or prunes, as my mother the word-mangler would say), my mother and aunt might find a sexual implication where I meant none. Thanking God for my ability to hold back those words, I said, "They need a drink."

"They don't serve drinks here," my mother said, getting the fact that I meant "drinks with booze." I was not surprised. My mother has not lost her uncanny ability to gauge everyone's mood.

"Are you warm enough, Jo?" my aunt asked, and my mother said she was, much to my relief. Aunt Millie has a mind like a steel trap, and during our last diner visit I had neglected to bring along a sweater and light scarf for Mom. My cousin Barbara, who packs her car with every necessity, had to return to the parking lot and retrieve these items from her stash.

But today I had succeeded in remembering not only a light cardigan but a fashionable scarf that I fastened—perhaps too tightly in my haste—about my mother's neck. Mom grimaced, and, instead of feeling badly, I was annoyed.

Okay, so I'm not perfect, I wanted to say under my breath. But looking at my two cousins, who would move heaven and earth for their mom, I felt surly and inferior. Where could that darn server be anyway?

A few minutes later, the server arrived and took our order. She smiled at our moms, as strangers so often did. To my relief, no one asked about booze. Not because I would have begrudged my cousins a drink, but because I would have felt guilty about my part in their having a need for one. My mother decided on pancakes and coffee, with a bit of help from me. Aunt Millie presented more of a challenge.

"What do I want, Barbara?" she said, and I inwardly sighed. I knew that if I were Barbara and Lois, I would be tempted to put my head in my hands and weep. This happened during every meal out with "the ladies." Barbara and Lois would tick through a multitude of choices before my aunt would settle on one. None of us were spring chickens, and yet we were consistently challenged and drained in so many ways. Having your parent live past the age of, say, eighty-five is a double-edged sword. For my cousins and me, the worry about finances and the decision-making concerning health care became paramount in our lives. Having waited until our thirties to have children, we had barely finished making decisions regarding where to raise them and what schools they would attend before we faced another issue: where would our aging parents live, and which doctors and hospitals should we take them to? Between us, we have racked up countless miles and hours thanks to doctor visits, hospital stays, evaluations of local apartments and, later, nursing homes, visits to local diners and restaurants to "get the girls out a little," Medicare and Medicaid applications, etcetera. We have had the blessing of our mothers' love and affection and wisdom for far longer than we most likely deserved. But it would be disingenuous to say it came without a price.

Compared with my cousins Barbara and Lois, I had a somewhat easier time of it. With the onset of dementia, my mother became easier to please. She stopped being the constant roundabout critic she used to be. As in, "Are you sure you want to wear that sweater, Mary Ann?" Or, even better, "I know you like your outfit, but maybe you should check yourself in a full-length mirror."

Dementia had another interesting effect on my mom, who always used to think a step ahead in a scattered and disruptive way. I always felt like I lost her midway through any conversation. With the onset of dementia, she began to focus her energy on being in the moment. While cruelly sweeping away details of her day-to-day routine and aspects of self-care, dementia also cleared the endless particles of distraction as well. There is no longer any need for my mother to read *The Power of Now*, not that she had ever been so inclined. Mom's mental clarity is on the downswing, but her level of satisfaction is still on the upswing.

"That's good, Josephine, you're cutting your own pancake," my aunt said approvingly.

"Should I be cutting my own pancake?" my mother asked. She is on a constant quest for affirmation.

"Yes, that's good," my aunt said, and I breathed a sigh of relief.

My cousins always cut up my aunt Millie's food, and my aunt once suggested I do the same for Mom.

"She needs to do some things on her own, it's good for her," I said, defending myself. Was it stubbornness on my part, or a real desire to help my mother stay somewhat independent that compelled me to not comply with my aunt's request? I was never one hundred percent sure whether my decisions regarding my mother's care were unselfish or not. As my friend Harry reminded me, having provided in-home care for his own mother with dementia, guilt and self-doubt are huge parts of the equation.

Confusion is a part of it as well, and not just in the mind of the victim. For a while I was confused about why Mom was behaving differently. She was scattered, yet willful. And it took me a while to get my head out of the sand and search for answers. Dealing with my mother's diagnosis of dementia consumed me, and I never gave much thought to how my aunt and cousins must have felt.

My aunt, especially, would kindly try to commiserate. "I forget things, too," she would say when I explained why my mother was not engaging in much conversation during visits and particularly during phone calls. My aunt is strong-willed and faith-filled, and I admire her for both of those qualities. I think she thought perhaps she could will or pray my mother's dementia away. I can't say that I blame her, and I surely wish she could have.

I never thought overly much about the toll my mother's downfall was taking on her only sister. They were lifelong best friends, and I am sure it was hard for my aunt to accept the loss, albeit partial, of their deep camaraderie. Mom now needed an explanation of Aunt Millie's jokes and couldn't remember recent events. The only safe place was the distant past, and my aunt Millie was always willing to go there with Mom. She was a true marvel, and my hero. Of all the people who had to swallow my mom's diagnosis, Aunt Millie was the bravest.

Now, on this afternoon at the diner, my aunt once again spoke of the past. My mother was drawn in, and—although she said little—I could tell she was entertained. In no time the two sisters were laughing and smiling, and their joy made them seem much younger than their years. My cousins relaxed as well, and we enjoyed listening to the ladies. My mother concentrated mightily on her conversation with Aunt Millie and eating her pancake. Unlike the old Josephine, the new Josephine was not commenting that the coffee was not hot enough or remarking that the waitress was too old to be wearing such a short skirt or that the vinyl on the booth was cracked or that cold air was blowing on us or that the whole place could use a "freshening." She was, finally and blessedly, just enjoying herself.

After warm goodbyes and a line or two of the sisters song, compliments of Aunt Millie, Mom and I returned home. John helped me get Mom back up to her room for a nap.

"Did you have fun with your sister?" I asked.

"I think so," Mom answered. "We were at the diner, right?"

"Yes, Mom, and you had pancakes," I answered, and Mom's eyes brightened.

"I like pancakes," she said.

"You like naps, too," I said, feeling mightily worn out and in need of one myself. I knew that upon awakening from her nap, Mom would remember almost nothing of our visit to the diner. Well, maybe the fact that "the girls" needed a cocktail. It's funny the things that are retained.

I used to wonder if these outings were worth all the effort, considering the fact that Mom rarely remembered them. But now I know it's not about remembering the moment.

It's about being in the moment.

Mom's younger brother, Gabe, adores his two sisters and is adored by them. My mother's diagnosis of dementia hit him hard. That is why, when Mom lived with me, I tried to have her talk to him on the phone only when she was having an "on" day.

During one phone call, my plan went awry. It started out promisingly enough, and then things took a downturn.

This is what I heard on Mom's end.

"Hi, Gabe, how are you? How is Marie, and how are the children?"

I strained to hear Uncle Gabe fill Mom in on the details of his family's health and travels and doings. I heard him ask how she was feeling. But my mom can only handle so much telephone conversation—usually about five to ten minutes' worth—before handing the phone back to me.

"Wow, she sounds great," Uncle Gabe said to me with relief.

"Doesn't she?" I said, and then I began feeling at loose ends. Although it happened on a regular basis, I was always somewhat thrown off when my mother handed me the phone in the middle of a conversation with Aunt Millie, Uncle Gabe, or my dad's sister Betty.

"Do you want to say goodbye to Mom?" I asked my uncle impulsively before realizing this could be a loaded question. The goodbye could go well, or it could add to Mom's anxiety and confusion. I was almost hoping my uncle would say no, but, of course, he did not.

"Sure!" said Uncle Gabe, buoyed by his productive conversation with Mom.

I handed Mom the phone, and to my surprise she didn't ask me any questions about what to say to her brother. She was the picture of confidence.

"Hi, Gabe, how are you?" Mom said. "How is Marie, and how are the children?"

To my relief, after an initial half second of surprise, I heard my uncle patiently reiterate everything he'd told my mother just moments before.

And that, in a nutshell, is brotherly love.

Chapter Twenty-Seven

Bad Santa

AS MOM'S CAREGIVER, I VIEWED DEMENTIA AS A TWISTED version of Santa Claus: chock-full of surprises, and not all of them good.

Just when it seemed like her thought process was skiing along on a steady but slow downhill run, it hit a mogul. She would get a burst of mental energy that lifted her up for a little while, then deposited her back down roughly and much lower on the slope.

These temporary upswings, when Mom was "on" and back to her old self, were illuminating, frustrating, draining, and heart-breaking all at the same time.

Most times, Mom was not able to manage the thought process or mechanics behind much of her daily routine. I prepared her meals, reminded her to eat, and assisted her with dressing and bathing.

This sounds tougher than it was. I had it easier than many caregivers. The blessing in disguise was that Mom slept much of the day, freeing up my early mornings and afternoons for writing, shopping, and daily walks. Her usual wake-up time, if left to her own devices, was around eleven a.m. I would check in on her beginning around ten a.m., but a sure sign that she was ready to get out of bed was her signature cough. I used to think she did not want to startle me by yelling to let me know that she was ready to begin her day. But now I think on some days she couldn't come up with the words. With dementia, you never really know for sure.

Mom's first "on" day occurred after she had lived with us for over six months. I was still trying to understand and accept her dementia diagnosis but had resigned myself to the fact that she would never be the woman she once was. Then one day while I was working on my laptop in the family room, Mom dressed herself and walked down the stairs leading to the kitchen. She surprised me as I left my workspace in the family room to fetch myself yet another cup of coffee.

"Mary Ann, this is where I am supposed to be, right?"

It was eight-thirty a.m. And she hadn't eaten a meal at the kitchen table in weeks.

"Uh, yes!" I managed, trying to keep my voice even and reassuring. I had no idea what had happened. I thought it was a miracle or an amazing reaction to the new "brain food" vitamins I had recently purchased.

"She's back!" I excitedly told John, phoning him at work to share the good news. That day, Mom worked on her crocheting, asked me to locate and deliver her makeup bag (which I fortunately hadn't tossed out), and asked on-point questions of me, my husband, and my kids. She even enjoyed lengthy phone conversations with her sister Millie and brother Gabe.

In three days, it was over, and we were back to square one. Actually, negative one.

I did a little research. These cycles are actually a dementia "thing." As if dementia, with its cruelty and capriciousness, needed to throw anything else into the mix.

Even though I learned to expect these cycles, they still messed with my head. The first day of Mom being "on" was always a bit rough. It sent her into a manic state and threw me off when she was not content to sleep most of the day away. She was agitated, overly talkative, and a bit demanding. Well, not demanding so much as asking for things that I had shamefully misplaced. Who knew she would want to crochet again, and where the heck did I put her crochet bag? It ate at me, this guilt, and wore me out.

During one "on" day, I was thrown a curveball in addition to the usual angst. The first day that Mom was "on" was the same day I had planned a visit to her doctor for a follow-up examination. Mom was a lot easier to manage in her usual state of confusion. I had no idea how I was going to make this doctor's visit happen. Fortunately, I was handed two lifelines.

The first was from my friend Margie, who had asked the day before if she could swing by with lunch for the two of us. Sweetly, she offered to bring something for Mom as well.

"No, don't worry," I said. "She doesn't have a big appetite these days. I'll just make her a cheese sandwich."

The next morning, after I realized that Mom was beginning an "on" phase, I sent a text to Margie. I asked if she could not only bring a sandwich for Mom, but stay after lunch and help me maneuver Mom through the garage and into my car for the doctor's appointment. I knew that an "on" Mom would be filled with questions, and I would be overwhelmed and exhausted.

I sure could use a helping hand, I thought. Unusual for me. I like to be in control. To my relief, Margie responded with a "yes!" almost immediately.

Margie was her usual solicitous and reliable self when, after lunch, she did the favor I had asked and helped me get Mom through a deluge of rain into the front seat of the Toyota. Thanks to Margie's mindfulness and skill with an umbrella, not a drop of rain touched Mom. Mom was appreciative of my efforts and Margie's help especially, but seemed more apprehensive than usual. Almost feisty. "Full of piss and vinegar," as my dad used to say. (He would know—under his quiet gentlemanly demeanor, he often was exactly like this.)

When we were preparing to leave the house, Mom called me out when I grabbed the wrong coat—mine—and tried to put it on her before realizing my mistake.

"Oh, jeez," I said, running back upstairs to fetch hers from her bedroom closet—where I had put it just days before so I wouldn't make the mistake I just had.

My mother continued to berate me as I put her own jacket on.

"Mary Ann was being silly," Margie said in her cheerful sing-song voice. I knew Margie was trying to diffuse the tension in the air, and I appreciated it. Still, I was annoyed and embarrassed.

I received my second lifeline before pulling out of the drive-way when John called me. "I'm in Red Bank, pretty close to the doctor's office," he said. "I'll meet you in his parking lot and help you get your mom to and from the appointment." I was greatly relieved.

Once we were finally on our way, Mom asked her usual question: "How far away is the doctor?"

"It's a short drive, but you can close your eyes if you want to," I answered, knowing her purpose. That's the thing about being in the dance long enough. You instinctively know your partner's next move.

Uncharacteristically, my mother opened her eyes instead of dozing off and began a conversation.

"Was that your friend Carol who helped us?"

"No, it was my friend Margie."

"Do I know her?"

"I think you've met her a few times before. She's very nice, isn't she?"

"Yes. She has three children, right?"

"No, just one. A very nice daughter."

"Oh, hmm." Mom sounded disappointed.

"What's wrong?" I responded quickly and defensively. "One daughter can be more than enough, you know."

"No, it's sad."

"Really?" I said, and I must have sounded annoyed.

"Not for your friend—for her daughter. She might be lonely."

I took in that statement and tried to form a response. Mom spoke again before I did.

"You had lots of cousins, though," she said hopefully.

"Yes, I did, Mom. I was lucky. I wasn't lonely."

Now it was Mom's turn to be quiet.

I swung my car into the parking lot, and John quickly arrived and parked next to me. As usual, Mom was thrilled to see him. "My favorite son-in-law," she often jokes.

With John's help and at the nurse's direction, I deposited my mother into the examining room, bypassing the dreaded waiting room.

"She can sit in the chair," the nurse instructed, but I was already headed for the examining table. "The chair is fine for this visit," the nurse said again, and I grabbed Mom's elbow and clumsily doubled back to the chair.

"Well, where am I sitting, the chair or the table?" Mom said in a voice that sounded at once irritated and superior.

I flinched, wounded, and I realized where I had heard that exact tone of voice before. It was from my father, addressing Mom when he was agitated and confused in a doctor's office. Funny, it had never bothered me as I stood looking on as an observer. But I recalled my mother's mouth clenching into a frown when it happened. It dawned on me her feelings were hurt, but she just pushed on as though nothing happened. She was a trouper.

Once we were seated and alone, with me on the examining table at Mom's insistence—"Give your feet a rest," another very Dad-like missive—Mom began again with the rapid-fire questions and comments.

"The doctor is taking a long time to come in here. She must be busy."

"It's a he, Mom. You've been seeing him for four years."

"I have? Well, is he nice?"

"Very nice."

"This place looks a little weird, though."

I had to laugh. I love Mom's doctor, I really do. But his office setup, in the large bottom floor of a sprawling split-level home, leaves me ill at ease. Even the examining table I was sitting on was covered with a silky but thick burgundy fabric covered with gold pineapple designs. Repurposed draperies from the house above us, perhaps?

Mom maintained her rapid-fire delivery of comments and questions throughout the seemingly endless wait, which ended up being thirty-plus minutes. I felt tired and concerned that John was losing work time while sitting in the waiting room. I also suspected that with Mom being very "on," I would not be in charge during this particular visit.

The doctor knocked and entered. Although his office space is quirky, he is decidedly not. He is always sharply dressed, well-spoken, polite, thoughtful, and sharp as a tack. Almost immediately he was aware of my mother's change in demeanor.

She answered all the questions he asked her directly, which is usually my role. Then she quizzed me about my answers to the ones he asked *me*.

"Wait, what kind of pill did you say you are giving me every other day?"

"Mom, what you don't know won't hurt you," I replied, not wanting to get into a discussion.

Mom laughed gamely, but I could tell she was put out. The doctor checked her blood pressure ("Excellent") and her heart ("Still the heart murmur, of course, but we're not worried about it right now").

At one point the doctor prepared my mother for a blood test, and I felt a bit faint. I don't react well when witnessing blood tests, and I know that they are more painful for Mom, due to the nerve damage caused by her diabetes. I was almost swooning and tried to shield my eyes. I could see Mom was distracted by the strange furnishings of the exam room ("Can we please move past it?" I wanted to scream in my agitated state), and she seemed unaware of what was about to take place. For some reason I felt compelled to warn her myself before he could say anything.

"You're gonna feel a pinch, Ma!" I yelled, sounding like Dorothy in "The Golden Girls."

Mom was quiet for a minute, and I think the doctor sighed with resignation. Mom and I are a sideshow at times.

Mom frowned and looked at me. "Why would you pinch me?" she asked, and the doctor took his opportunity to insert the needle while she was distracted.

"Ow!" she yelled, and I swooned. Luckily I was sitting down and able to rest my head in my hands.

"Are you okay?" Mom yelled.

"Yes, stay still!" I yelled back in a muffled voice.

Get me out of here, the doctor most likely thought. But he remained as cool as a cucumber.

"You're fit as a fiddle," the doctor announced at the end of the visit, and Mom's listening skills suddenly lost their steam. Either that, or she just wanted me to reiterate.

"I'm what?" she asked, turning to me.

"You're as healthy as a horse," I said, too loudly, and Mom frowned.

"That sounds terrible," she said.

The doctor intervened. "Josephine, you are doing very well," he said, and she smiled sweetly.

"Has she been agitated?" the doctor asked me, confidentially but just a touch too loudly. Years of listening intently to conversations in order to make up for my father's lack of good hearing has made Mom's skills sharper over the years. Dammit.

Mom was on this like a terrier with a plush toy.

"Am I *what*? *What* did he say?"

The doctor stiffened up and reddened, and I waved discreetly but dismissively. He moved on to the next question. I was disappointed to have lost the moment but figured that if Mom's agitation continued, I could just phone the office and ask for advice. I doubted that I would have to, since her "on" phases last three days at the most and her off phases, while disappointing, brought with them a measure of calm.

The conversation and questions continued on the ride home.

"Is that doctor married?"

"I don't know, Mom."

"Hmm, I wonder."

"I don't think he told us either way."

"Maybe he should have."

"I don't know. I mean, it's not necessary."

"Yes, but it would be nice to know."

"I guess. Why, are you interested?"

"Well, yes, I am," she responded firmly, and I knew that she had missed my intended meaning. She was not *interested*. Certainly not in a romantic way. Just nosy. The way I used to be, before I recently decided that caring overly much about other people's lives was a waste of time. I now had enough going on under my own roof.

Mom continued. "Well, I think he is married with three children."

"Could be," I said. This was not Mom being delusional, which she wasn't even on her off days. This was Mom wanting to give the nice doctor a wife and three children. Mom has always wanted to give everyone children, preferably more than one (ahem).

She is currently obsessed with the number three. "Should I take three sips of this coffee?" she often asked in the morning.

"Sure," I would say, because it was easier than arguing.

Instead of heading off to bed for a nap when we arrived home, Mom asked for a cup of coffee. I delivered the coffee to her tray table in the living room, and she asked if she could take three sips.

Later that night, after eating dinner with John and me in the dining room instead of in her bedroom on the tray table, she was full of conversation while we watched TV. This was a very nice change of pace. I missed watching TV with Mom, as she usually preferred to stay in her room where it was warmer.

At nine-thirty, Mom began to nod off on the sofa.

"Why don't you go to bed, Mom?" John suggested.

Mom appeared peeved. "Well, what time is it?" she asked.

"Nine-thirty," John answered, always truthful.

"That's too early," she said. I predicted what would come next with one hundred percent certainty.

"Are *you* going to bed?" she said, looking at me.

"No, I am going to bed at ten," I lied. I wanted a few minutes of alone time.

"Then I'll go to bed at ten, too," she said as though the matter was decided. And, actually, it was.

But, of course, I ended up still in her bedroom at a quarter past ten, performing the little tasks associated with a successful nighttime sendoff for Josephine. And I was peeved. So I behaved peevishly.

"I was hoping to be in bed by now, Mom," I said, immediately regretting the words. Mom was having an "on" day. Why was I stealing her thunder?

"Well, why?" she answered. "Can't you sleep late tomorrow?"

Humor has always been a useful tool for my parents and me. We employed it liberally to get through the tough times and enjoy the good times even more. I always pray that dementia does not steal my mother's sense of humor. So far, so good.

"Like you do," I said, and smiled meaningfully.

"I always sleep late, don't I?" she said, laughing. "Why is that?"

My heart skipped a beat.

"I don't know," I responded, and because I was laughing, she laughed too. That is just what we do. "Smile and the world smiles with you, cry and you cry alone," my father would remind me at the most inopportune times. Such as when I was actually crying. A real softie, that one.

Mom, though, *is* a softie. Or at least she can be. "It's too bad you can't sleep late, too," she said thoughtfully.

With thoughts of alone time foremost in my mind, I told her to get into bed so I could turn off her bedroom lamp. I then made a shameless beeline for the family room, where I would use the DVR to retrace key points in my favorite TV drama.

"Good night," Mom yelled after me.

"Good night, Mom," I shouted back.

"I love you," Mom yelled.

"I love you," I shouted back louder, since I was already almost in the family room. Where, despite the distraction provided on-screen, my mind wandered to the truth of the matter.

If past cycles were any indication, I was gambling on the fact that my mother (and I) could expect to have an even better day tomorrow. Tomorrow, I told myself, Mom will be clear-headed, alert, and energetic. She will wake up early. She will get herself down the stairs and into the kitchen, but tomorrow I won't be surprised to see her. Seated at the kitchen table, she will urge me not to fuss with fixing an English muffin for her breakfast; cereal is just fine. I will prepare the muffin anyway, and she will be pleasantly surprised and she will thank me. I will be pleas-antly surprised and a bit shocked to see that while I returned to the family room to do some work on my laptop, she washed her cup and dish and placed them carefully in the dish drain. She will return to her room and put on her makeup and straighten the comforter on her bed with military precision, in a way that I can never manage to. She will dress herself in a pretty blouse and skirt, and she will appear even more beautiful than she usually does. She will watch game shows in the family room while I sit nearby and write, and she and I will have pleasant conversation on and off throughout the day.

She will nap in the afternoon, and she and John and I will enjoy our dinner together. She will praise the meal and thank me for it. We will head to the family room and watch our game shows and comedies. This time, Mom will not talk through them. She will be far less agitated, and our conversation will be on and off but pleasant. I will help Mom get ready for bed, and we will find something to laugh about—maybe the fact that she is struggling to get her "stupid" diaper on, or that it is a good thing John is downstairs and oblivious to her bedtime changing routine.

"He would never be the same," she will joke. And we will both head off to bed. She happily, me a bit anxious. Because sometimes Mom got three good days, and sometimes just two. I usually didn't know what to expect. But this time my gut was telling me that it would be just two. As it turned out, I was right.

On day three, I heard Mom rustling around in the bathroom. It was well after nine a.m.

"Mom, are you okay?" I asked.

"Yes, I'm fine," she answered. But her voice sounded dull and not strong and sure, the way it had been for the past two days.

"Are you going back to bed?" I asked.

"Yes," she answered. "You're waking me up at six o'clock for dinner, right?"

And just like that, I knew she was gone again. And, shamefully, part of me was relieved to be able to return to our usual routine. But the bigger part of me would go through the process of missing my mom's company. Yet again.

Remember what Mom said during our car ride to the doctor's office? The part about the only daughter being lonely?

Sometimes it *is* true. But so is something else.

I am also lucky.

Dementia may be a bad Santa, but my mom was a good one. One year, when we lived in Union City, Mom decided to do the "modern" thing and order all of my Christmas toys from the Sears catalog. As of December 24th, they hadn't arrived.

So, in the late afternoon of Christmas Eve 1962, my mother dropped me off with my aunt Millie and braced herself for a freezing cold and blustery excursion. She walked to the corner and took the bus. She managed to find the only toy story open; it was on Bergenline Avenue in North Bergen, a few towns and more than a few miles away. She did all the shopping and wrapping herself, since Dad worked the night shift.

I awoke on Christmas morning to a bevy of gifts, including that doll Mom had spied originally at the Sears store. As it turned out, I ended up loving that rosy-cheeked, blue-eyed doll and her pink dress and crinkly honey-blonde hair.

But not nearly as much as I love my mom.

Chapter Twenty-Eight

Banking on the System

"YOU'RE NOT A CRIMINAL," MY FRIEND LESLIE ASSURED ME during our morning stroll.

Leslie and I had been walking together in the mornings for about fifteen years. Her daughter and mine were in the same grade at school, and our discussions centered around family and weekend plans and our shared philosophy on life ("All's well that ends well!"). We sometimes had some serious discussions about life-altering events. But neither of us had ever shed a tear.

I was the first to crack.

I had decided to apply for Medicaid on my mother's behalf. And the required ten-year financial lookback was giving me fits.

I usually didn't drag friends into my "mama drama," figuring that they had enough going on in their own lives. But on this particular day, I was feeling helpless. Applying represented a lot of work on my part, and also brought home the fact that I was beginning to consider nursing home care for my mom—and I needed Medicaid to help cover costs and make it happen. I felt compelled to apply for state aid for a number of reasons.

Things had been humming along fairly well for me and Mom up to a certain point. And then we hit some bumps. Mostly me getting tired of putting Mom's needs ahead of my own. My mother's presence had become disruptive to the point where it was affecting my ability to interact with my kids when they arrived home for short or extended stays. Despite my best efforts, I found myself getting fed up. I had been told that I would eventually end up resenting my mom after moving her in, and at the time I couldn't imagine it happening. But here it was.

Another reason that I applied for state aid was this—I needed to plan for what would happen in the event that John outlived me. Or in the event that Mom outlived both of us. A sobering thought, for sure, but not out of the realm of possibility.

Unlike the conversation that Mom and I had about my dad years before, the conversation I had with John about Mom went like this:

"Promise me that if something happens to me, you'll put Mom in a nursing home."

John hesitated for a moment. He always wants to be everyone's knight in shining armor. And often he is just that. But I could see his eyes darken as reality set in.

"Okay," he said, grimacing. Like my mom, he doesn't give up easily. But I needed to set the wheels in motion.

A ten-year lookback into my parents' finances was bound to be painful. Like a bookkeeper called into question, I simply was not sure where the money went. The small windfall from the sale of my parents' home had gone largely into their rent and living expenses and with more than a bit of nail-biting on my part.

"Don't worry, your money will last as long as you will," John had assured my parents back in 2002.

It seemed like yesterday. My parents were not interested in purchasing a condo, and my dad did not want to apply for any veteran's health benefits. In 2002, Dad was eighty-four years old and Mom was seventy-five. My gambler's instincts were betting on the fact that they would have less than ten years left.

"Save that for the younger guys who are doing their duty now," Dad said when I offered to do the paperwork for veteran's health benefits. Case closed. I knew not to push. The one time I had seen my dad get anywhere near emotional was when he talked to me about the terrible treatment of Vietnam veterans when they returned home.

As I dried my eyes and Leslie and I passed the familiar landmarks of our morning walk, she reassured me by speaking with authority about the difficulties and problems associated with "the system." Having worked in health care for years, Leslie knew her stuff. But what she didn't know was this. The reason I had been crying was partly my fault.

I had stupidly assumed that the ten-year lookback I had been warned about required me to procure and deliver *all* of my parents' bank statements for the past ten years. I hadn't been told otherwise. But I hadn't done my research or asked around before my first visit to the Medicaid office. When I handed a sheaf of checking and savings account statements to the person taking my Medicaid application information, he patiently leafed through them and announced that some were missing.

"You need the quarterly bank statements, not the ones from every month of the year," he informed me. "And some of the quarterly statements are not here."

My shoulders sagged. I left there feeling sad and unaccomplished and stupid. Within a few weeks I received a letter outlining which quarterly statements were missing, and I brought it to the bank. Working with the same bank manager, I retrieved all of the missing statements. Well, almost all of them, as I discovered when I returned home. I went through the list of twenty missing statements and realized that eight of them were still AWOL. I am ashamed to say that I began to cry. I visited the bank again and was told that there might be a problem retrieving the missing statements, since they were issued when the bank itself had changed hands. I flushed with aggravation and shame when I recalled that my parents had carefully saved all of their financial documents, and I had most likely thrown them away. I left the bank with nothing tangible, just a promise that the bank manager would do his best to help me and would call as soon as the statements came in. But after a few days, I started to get panicky.

"I can come to the bank with you to ask for those statements again if you want," Leslie said. I almost wept with gratitude.

"Let's go right after our walk," I said, feeling the excitement and promise of having an ally, and a savvy and well-spoken one at that.

"Oh, no," she corrected. "We need to go home and get dressed in office clothes. That's how you get the best service."

The truth and challenge of this statement struck me like a thunderbolt. I'd been so down. Not only had I not thought about dressing up for good service, I had not been feeling worthy of anyone going out of their way for me. I took Leslie's advice. Wearing black slacks and a gray sweater, I no longer felt in need of her assistance at the bank. I had an invisible ally, and that was good enough for me.

I can't say whether it was definitely due to the change in my thinking from defeatist to deserving, but everything regarding my application turned around after that. I was able to retrieve the information from the bank with the help of a new manager that I truly connected with. I was able to explain charges and withdrawals that had been flagged in my almost-monthly correspondence with Medicaid, and to do so honestly and without feeling like I wanted to stick my head in the sand (as I had been). And I was able to write explanatory letters to Medicaid telling the truth but also protecting myself.

"Yes, I have made some mistakes with record-keeping," I admitted. "But can we please keep this approval process moving along?" In other words, I prevailed. Not perfectly, but imperfectly. And that was good enough.

On my second visit to the state Medicaid office, I sat in the waiting room clutching a shiny black embossed leather briefcase holding all of the necessary documents. I was showered, dressed nicely, and confident. I shuddered when I thought about my first visit just weeks before. As I waited for my number to be called, I had noticed a tall and smoky-smelling woman wearing a house dress. She walked past the waiting area and approached the representative standing at a counter behind a glass window.

"I need to know why my food stamps benefit was cut," she said through the hole in the glass.

The representative studied the letter the woman pushed through a small slot. I could tell by her demeanor that the tall lady meant business, but the representative seemed unworried.

"Well, it says here that you had a higher benefit because someone was living with you," she explained, a bit too loudly. "He reported to us that he left your residence, and now your benefit is lower because it's for just one person."

The tall woman huffed. "I had that higher amount before he came to live with me," she said. "Why is it suddenly lower?"

The representative pursed her lips and directed the woman to a set of cubicles out of range of sight and hearing.

Tsk, tsk, I said to my superior self without an ounce of pity. I had decided years ago that the system was broken. I complained about money coming out of my paycheck to help "them," whoever "they" were. But here was this smoky woman. And I knew who she was. She was one of "them." And she had been getting overpaid to boot. Good for that guy, whoever he is, I thought. He let the authorities know that she was abusing the system.

I never thought to ask myself this burning question: if she's one of "them," what does that make me and my mom?

The experience a few weeks later of needing a helping hand and a nonjudgmental attitude and getting them from Leslie turned my thinking around.

Who was I to say that the woman in the house dress didn't enter that office asking herself the very same questions that were bouncing around in my head the day I observed her?

What the heck happened? Why is my life such a mess, and where did the money go?

And here's another thing to consider.

Unlike me, that woman had most likely filled the paperwork out correctly and provided the correct information the first time around.

Lesson in humility? Check.

Chapter Twenty-Nine

Any Port in a Storm

I WAS AT A NEARBY DRUGSTORE, PERUSING THE OFFER-ings in the way of SPF-rich daytime skin creams. The effects of sun exposure and aging had convinced me that I needed to up my everyday protection from fifteen to thirty. Well, that and the fact that I was bored and feeling at loose ends.

Drugstore shopping has been a somewhat inexpensive diversion for me for years, and at no time had I craved it more than when Mom lived with me. Too much time spent in the Josephine Zone sent me running for the nearest collection of nail polish, shampoo, conditioner, skin and body care, and makeup. I tried to tell myself that it was an affordable pleasure, but in truth I averaged twenty to forty dollars per trip. I avoided thinking about it overly much or adding it all up in my head. I really did try to not buy anything, but to me that felt like a failed hunting expedition. Like I was some sort of cavewoman and my family was expecting me to drag home a felled mammoth or something along those lines.

I shopped at the nearby Duane Reade drugstore so often when I was an advertising copywriter in New York City, my male coworkers ribbed me about it.

"You have to come back to work," my boss once told me during a phone call when I was on maternity leave. "The Duane Reade is on the verge of closing for good."

I laughed, but he had a point. I didn't end up returning to work. And the Duane Reade did close.

When Mom moved in, my cosmetics-based escapism escalated. I sat up in my bed every night basking in the glow of my tablet and waiting expectantly for the cosmetics discussion and review sites to load. I compared face creams and foundations and shampoos in a frenzied fashion as though I were getting paid to do so. My hard work paid off as I cracked the Internet code of the cosmetics-crazed. IMO means "in my opinion," and HG means "Holy Grail." Wow, who knew? Sometimes, pathetically, I would click on a reviewer's name and go into her history to find out what products she was using in, say, 2009.

Aw, that's the year Veronica graduated eighth grade. And yes, that's the year Bond No. 9 perfume was sooooo popular—whatever happened to Bond No. 9? It sounds like a frivolous activity, but it had deeper implications. What I was really thinking was, Where did the time go, and why didn't I make the most of it? Everyone else seems so productive and accomplished. What is wrong with me?

Cosmetics sites became, for me, a strange combination of research and self-flagellation. And they somehow became a necessity when Mom lived with me.

I fessed up about my addiction one day to my no-nonsense, straight-shooting friends Carol and Hope. I feared they might advise me to ease up. Instead, they tossed me a lifeline.

"There's nothing wrong with that, as long as you're just using it to get you through a tough time," was the consensus.

I took this in and breathed a huge sigh of relief. So what if I needed a thumbs up or thumbs down on a foundation I was considering, or shopping for cosmetics to get me through the night? What was the harm in that? With my friends' help, I began to feel a lot less embarrassed by my newest must-haves.

I wish someone would have clued in the twenty-something sales clerk at the drugstore, though. On that evening, I was actually washed and fairly well dressed, thanks to the fact that I had just attended a play at the local grammar school. Still, I could see she was eyeing me suspiciously. She seemed to be following me. Perhaps I had knelt down one too many times in front of the "Sinful Colors" nail glaze display. But all of the colors were so pretty. And truthfully, as a middle-aged woman, part of me wants to be thought of as "sinful," something that I never would have considered in my very uptight late teens and twenties.

Despite the lovely display, I ended up deciding on none. "See? You can be economical!" I said silently, congratulating myself on a job well done.

I turned the corner and almost walked into the sales clerk. She snuck a glance at my hands, which were empty. Did she suspect that I had dropped one or two of the bottles of sinful color into the pockets of my Via Spiga rain coat? It's a sharp coat. Didn't I look like I could darn well afford one or two bottles of nail glaze costing only $1.99 each? Maybe she thought I was one of those people who shoplift for the thrill of it. Or drugstore-shop for the thrill of it. It was always possible I could sink lower.

Still, the watchful and cranky sales clerk was pissing me off. Didn't she know this was a big night out for me?

Don't rain on my parade, I thought, and I wanted to cry with pity for myself. Not for the first time. I knew I wasn't being fair to her. She was just doing her job. And she had no way of knowing that, with my diminished capacity to spend time and money, a trip to the drugstore felt like it could be in the same class as, say, a tropical getaway—not because I wanted it to, but because it had to.

Fed up, I decided to leave the store empty-handed. No felled mammoth this time. Nothing had been accomplished, except for my usual wasting of time.

During the car ride home, my Sirius radio station blared out "Two Tickets to Paradise."

And I thought once again about how ironic life can be.

Chapter Thirty

Elephant in the Room

IT TOOK TIME AND EFFORT TO OPEN MYSELF TO THE lifelines all around me. I had to reach into corners of my mind and parts of my soul that I did not even know existed. And for them to be drawn out, I needed to step outside of my former self and do some reinvention.

Up to that point, I'd lived a secure life. As an only child, I'd experienced my parents' constant worries about my safety. Because they worried so much, it freed me to worry less. I took some chances. Not crazy ones, but chances nonetheless. As I grew older and left my parents' home, I became more cautious. Traveling, socializing, exercising, and even working were all done in moderation. As a coworker once pointed out, "You never push yourself too hard." He was right. As an only child with aging parents, I felt a very real responsibility to keep myself alive and well for their sakes. My habit of staying safe only strengthened when I added other responsibilities, like my husband and two children, to the mix.

But when Mom was diagnosed with dementia, that "play it safe" attitude stopped working for me. Dementia isn't safe. It chews you up and spits you out. And that is true not only for the victim, but for the caregiver as well.

One afternoon, with Mom dozing upstairs, I settled on my sofa and became transfixed by a documentary entitled *The Alzheimer's Project*. I did not expect to be as moved and reassured as I was. I am not a research-oriented person, preferring to act on instinct and figure it all out later. I know this is not a good thing, but it is how I am wired.

But this documentary touched a chord with me. The stories validated my feeling that Mom and I were like a ship lost at sea, as well as the fact that we had switched our mother/daughter roles. And in one particular story—about a mother and daughter living on a small farm and beholden only to each other—I empathized with the mother's constant need for direction and validation and the daughter's worries about financial ruin due to the fact that she could no longer work full time. I cried as I watched these two women cling to each other like survivors on a desert island. It was then I realized that the isolation of dementia was affecting Mom and me as well.

Like the mother and daughter, Mom and I had been upended by dementia. Mom was sort of aware of being on the fringe of things. I was acutely aware of it. The documentary was a wake-up call for me. So much for circling the wagons. I needed to seek out more sources of support.

My search for new lifelines led to hidden treasures like a self-help guide at a store selling used books. The colorful cover attracted me, and something compelled me to pick it up; in its pages I learned to start finding my strength and my voice. Then there was a music video from a "90s Retrospective" summer TV show that compelled me to rediscover my love for grunge rock. I had forgotten how the outsider lyrics and attitude of the genre could soothe my soul. And while I had long considered myself not to be a fan of group exercise, I participated in a Zumba fundraiser for a close friend and began to attend evening classes twice a week. Instead of immediately saying "maybe" to invitations and trying to figure out an excuse later on, I began saying "yes" more often and trying to figure out a way to participate. My friends and family members who once hovered in the stratosphere while I concerned myself with more important things, like housework, became a more constant presence and the bedrock of my life. I had always considered us close, but now I realized I had barely been paying attention to them. They had always been there for me. I just hadn't even touched the surface of what they had to offer. And vice versa.

It was hard work to have real conversations instead of the "smooth speaking" and "lazy listening" I had been guilty of. But it was freeing to actually listen to what someone else was saying rather than worry about how to fill in the silent moments. I find it funny that when I began this process, I worried about being viewed as slow to react during conversations. Ironically, I had never worried about being disingenuous.

I found myself opening up not only to close friends and relatives, but also to acquaintances and even strangers. I began to learn about the lives of local cashiers and restaurant servers and service providers. Not just "How are you doing?" but deeper than that. I managed to remember that my favorite cashier at the local Acme had a young son, and I asked about him. I had never known that the husband and wife who ran the local stationery store were renters and not owners of their property and that they were being forced to vacate their space to make room for an upscale restaurant. The woman who punches in the numbers for my lottery ticket divorced her philandering husband and was trying to figure out life as a newly single mom.

Where had these people been? Always there, right there in front of me. I was the one with my head stuck in the sand. Or maybe with my nose in the air.

Consumed for years by my own needs and my own busy life, I knew none of it. Nor did I care to. I had approached the door of knowing many times but never reached out to turn the knob, thinking it would bring me added worry and responsibility. I was wrong. Turning that knob has been gratifying.

One of the people I became more honest with was my husband. I started placing my needs out there more often after good friends helped me realize that, with so much on my plate, it would be of great benefit to my sanity if I learned how to speak up more. One weekend I did speak up. I was sick to death of venturing out alone to buy pajama bottoms for my mother. Not only was I always unsure of her style (she is very fussy about prints), but I needed to shop for them often. I couldn't buy them online—Mom required a certain degree of softness (not too soft) and give. While living with us, Mom got confused and began throwing her pajama bottoms into the trash bin instead of the laundry hamper. I got wise when I opened up her dresser drawer one day and found only pajama tops. I glanced over to see her pajama bottoms lying in her trash bin.

"Mom, you've been throwing your pajama bottoms into the garbage pail instead of your hamper!"

"Why would I do *that*?"

"I don't know, but it has to stop. You can't do that anymore!"

"Okay, I'll try to remember. Now, what was it I'm doing wrong again?"

"Throwing your pajama bottoms into the garbage pail instead of your hamper!"

"Why would I do *that*?"

I am well aware that I could solve this problem by rooting around in Mom's trash bin more often. But on most days I just didn't have the nerve or the strength. Call me stupid, but I thought it made more sense to just stock up on pajama bottoms. I decided on this approach despite what always happened after bringing the prized pajama bottoms home. Due to my mother's lack of height but need for a large size, they almost always need to be hemmed. It was a production. It was, as my father would say, "Too much!"

I decided that I needed an ally, at least for the shopping part. I wanted it to be John. And I told him so, rather forcefully. Truth is, I've always had trouble separating assertion from aggression. As this was one of the first times I was assertively asking John to shop with me, I may have erred on the side of aggression. In any case, he readily agreed to my plan.

So there was John with a forced smile on his face as I browsed the offerings in our local Boscov's. I almost shrieked when I saw a full circular rack of "cropped" pajama pants in sizes from small to XXX-large. How had I missed these in the past? "No hemming!" flashed on and off in my head like a neon sign.

Although the bright colors were a departure for Mom, I grabbed a bunch, including one festooned with cartoon elephants wearing pink bows. The background was turquoise—the only bright color Mom favored—and elephants were the favorite animal of her beloved late sister-in-law Bernice.

I was almost giddy with excitement when I brought my stash of seven pajama bottoms to the register.

"These are *perfect!*" I informed the cashier, who appeared to be in her early sixties and was dressed beautifully. No elephants on *her* clothes. I felt compelled to explain myself while John looked away, discreetly pretending to not be associated with me.

"My mom will love the ones with the elephants, I think," I said. "She certainly loved her sister-in-law who loved elephants. And these are the perfect length, since my mother is not even five feet tall."

For a second, I thought this might be TMI, and John stopped staring in the other direction and stared at me with an alarmed expression. Oh no, I thought. John keeps his cards very close to the vest. He is not secretive as much as seriously reserved with strangers. Now we were both waiting for the cashier's reaction.

To my relief, the cashier's smile widened.

"So your mother is a small lady," she said. "And I am guessing she is a small lady with a big heart. A heart like these elephants."

I almost wept with gratitude. Talk about hitting the nail on the head.

"So you get it," I said, smiling as the cashier nodded. John was smiling, too.

The cashier's goodbye to us felt more like a blessing. We had entered the store feeling the burden of doing yet another something to take care of that one extra person in our house. We left feeling lighter than air.

Someone got it. For a little while, walking through that store and clutching our bag filled with pajama bottoms, life seemed normal and we felt hopeful. Dementia has a way of constantly pulling the rug out from under you and wearing you out. People who get it are like droplets of water that help to refill a depleted well of good intentions. I don't think they are aware of their effect or their power.

But now I am. And so is John.

Chapter Thirty-One

Shop Talk

I PLACED MY ITEMS ON THE BELT AT THE SHOPRITE, ADD-ing up the cost in my head. I had filled my cart with paper towels, toilet paper, mop heads, and a variety of cleaning agents after driving twenty minutes in the pouring rain to West Long Branch.

The cashier, a woman who appeared to be my age or just a touch older, said, "Looks like you're doing some spring cleaning."

"No," I said. "My mom lives with me."

I almost blushed, embarrassed by my candor. Perhaps I should have just nodded and agreed. But I had learned to tell the truth about my situation when I sensed I might be interacting with a kindred spirit who could commiserate with me. Nine times out of ten, my instincts were spot-on.

"Oh, I totally get it," the cashier said. She went on to tell me that she had cared for her mom for a few years. Then the conversation took a turn. "Then it just got to be too much," she continued. "I called my sister in California, and she made room in her home for my mom."

"That's wonderful," I said, feeling deflated. If I had pretty much reveled in my role as an only child while growing up—No sharing of toys! No sisters to come along and be prettier than me!—I was surely paying the piper now.

"Well," she said finally, "I hope you have your mother for many, many years to come."

I sighed, but managed a polite thank you. You phony, I thought. It was too much for you, but it's just fine for me? I grabbed my bags and left in a hurry.

During the drive home, I thought about the cashier's statement. There is so much inner turmoil involved in elder care. And conflicting statements made by sometimes well-meaning people only added to my angst.

"Good for you, keep up the good work and God bless; personally, it was too much for me."

A few weeks before, my friend Pat told me her mom had been diagnosed with dementia and had moved into Pat's home in northern New Jersey six months earlier. Pat also told me she had placed her mom in a nursing home recently and things were working out splendidly. She excitedly told me her mom was enjoying the food and the activities immensely. And Pat had been able to go back to work full-time. Emotionally and financially, things were looking up for her. "I wish you lived closer," Pat said. "Your mom could be in the same home as mine. But I know you can find an excellent facility near you."

I was moved by Pat's concern for me and mom and happy for her success. Somehow I couldn't see the same thing happening for me. This was partly because, for every story like Pat's, I'd heard plenty of statements like these:

"That's no way for your mom to finish her life, wasting away in a place like that."

"My friend put her mom in a home and sold all of her bedroom furniture. Her mom ended up hating the place, and two months later she was back in the house. And my friend, the poor thing, ended up buying a whole set of new furniture."

In the tug-of-war that was taking place in my brain as I drove home, Pat was winning. Mom had woken us up at four o'clock that morning, calling for me. She had clogged the toilet by using too much toilet paper. I found her in the bathroom standing in a huge puddle of water and staring at the now-overflowing toilet. John stayed up with us for over an hour, helping me get Mom cleaned up and handing me endless paper towels as I mopped the bathroom floor while he kept Mom occupied. He knew without asking that I was ready to snap at her for no good reason.

"I'm sorry, what did I do?" she kept asking. "Can I go back to bed?"

"No, Mom, Mary Ann has to clean you up first," he explained.

"Oh," Mom said. "What happened?"

When things were somewhat under control, I ordered John to bed. The man had had open-heart surgery at the age of fifty, and he worked endless hours in a demanding corporate position. I performed my cleanup duty.

"Oh," Mom said when I scrubbed her down with a washcloth containing cold water. She flinched, and I felt bad, but just for a second. Something had to give.

The next day, after my trip to the grocery store, I used my newly purchased supplies to clean any spots I had missed in the bathroom. Then I faced my weary husband. "I can't believe I managed to unclog the toilet by myself without calling a plumber," I said.

He smiled. I thought about my friend Pat's husband and how relieved he must have felt once his mother-in-law situation was squared away.

"How will we know when we're done?" I asked.

"I don't know," John answered. For the first time ever, he added, "But I think we're getting closer."

Chapter Thirty-Two

Fork in the Road

IN THE WINTER OF 2016, I SPENT A GOOD PORTION OF MY days running upstairs to see if Mom was asleep or awake. Most of the time she was asleep, and I was relieved. Avoidance had become the most-used item in my caregiver's tool belt. Mom and I were stuck in a vicious cycle. I was sad, and she was sad. It's hard for one depressed person to lift the other up. We were both worn out. Me, from losing Dad and from guilt over all the things I felt I had done wrong to get us into this mess. And Mom, from losing Dad and from old age and dementia and not sleeping at night. My sentence was self-imposed. Mom's was not.

Mom used to be at the center of things. Many of our relatives begged her and my dad to attend their many gatherings. Mom feared she and Dad would be in the way, and potential hosts had to jump through hoops to secure that "yes." It was worth it, as my parents were always fun to be with. "Thanksgiving and Christmas are coming up, and I sure hope your Mom says 'yes' right away this time," my mother-in-law Dolly would say as we enjoyed coffee at her kitchen table. I would sigh, knowing the first "no" was inevitable. Dolly had been willing to jump through hoops to be with my mom. And now I was doing everything in my power to get away from her.

I even dreaded waking Mom up for breakfast. "I know I was supposed to pray for someone or something last night, but I wasn't sure who or what," my bleary-eyed Mom would say almost every morning. "I lay there and lay there, trying to figure it out. Do you know what I was supposed to pray for? Or who?"

"No, I really don't," I would answer. "Everything is fine, there's no need to worry." I was too much inside my own head to help her out. That, and I knew she wouldn't remember anything I told her long enough to pray on it that night. I tried to remind myself that this was unkind, and that people with dementia deserve the courtesy of being told what is going on around them. Surely Mom was picking up on the negative vibe that permeated our existence. But I delivered only good news, and sparingly. I told myself she couldn't handle the whole truth. In reality, it was me who couldn't handle bothering to tell it to her.

I wasn't feeling or acting my best. Far from it. I felt like I was standing still while my friends were moving forward. They were sharpening their skills. Selling their artwork. Earning advanced degrees. Remodeling their homes. Traveling to Europe. Well, not all of my friends. But these were the stories I focused on. I was using any excuse to feel sorry for myself. One day I even stopped watching my beloved *Dr. Phil* because I realized his guests—undergoing all kinds of serious trouble—looked way better than I did.

A big part of me wished I had gotten a full-time job to help with the heavy college expenses and put Mom in a nursing home after Dad passed away in April 2013. I might not have felt great about that decision at the time, but there was also the possibility it would have worked out just fine. Mom wouldn't have been on her own for a year in the apartment. And I would have been more inclined to consider myself a productive member of society by bringing in a steady paycheck instead of the dribs and drabs of consulting work. "Are you expecting a check in the mail soon?" was a question from my husband that I learned to dread. John and our kids, to their credit, were totally supportive and understanding of the situation. John never asked me to choose between my mom and financial security. Greg and Veronica took out student loans without complaint and treated their grammy like a queen. I was the one falling apart at the seams.

One evening around this time, I was invited to join three high school friends for dinner. Eileen, Cindy, and Diane are down-to-earth and honest and smart and funny. Many years ago my mother wished I could be a cheerleader and one of the popular girls in high school, and surely that was because she wanted to live through me. Josephine was shy and learning-challenged and quit high school in her junior year after having an unspectacular time of it, academically and socially. Of course my heart bleeds for her. My mother is kind and funny and talented and street-smart and generous. She deserved better. But I couldn't be the one to deliver it to her vicariously years later. I had my own life to live, and mine involved making friends who would get me through the tough times as well as the good times. These three ladies were those friends, and I was really looking forward to spending time with them.

"I love getting together with friends who have known you forever, because you don't need to fill them in on your history and explain yourself," said Eileen as soon as we were seated at a table in our favorite Italian restaurant in Westfield.

I smiled. Eileen was right. Cindy and Diane and I got together fairly regularly, but Eileen had a lot more going on, including working weekends in her successful bakery. Cindy and Diane and I were happy to be finally catching up in person with Eileen, and I figured beforehand that her goings-on would be the main focus. I was surprised when Eileen turned the tables after our first half hour or so of conversation.

"So, how's the situation with your mom?" Eileen asked, focusing her blue-lavender eyes on me.

I hesitated. Eileen's gaze let me know she meant business and none of my usual BS was going to do.

"Well, let me ask you this: are you lying awake in bed at night with your heart pounding?" Eileen continued after I made no response. "And are you half-wishing that you *would* have a heart attack just so someone would take care of *you* for a change?"

"Yes!" I admitted. This was one of my darkest secrets, and I could not believe I had shared it.

But Eileen was nothing if not understanding. She was one of the kindest girls in our high school class. Cindy and Diane halted their conversation and gave me a quick sideways glance. I feared judgment for a split second, then I scolded myself. These were my best friends, and when I put aside my insecurity to tune in to their vibe, I could tell—without any exchange of words between us—that it was one of concern. They, too, had cared for sick parents years ago. I felt a weight come off my shoulders.

Eileen spoke on reassuringly, and I focused on her beautiful face while I tried not to cry. Eileen had not only guessed my innermost thoughts, but she also understood. I had forgotten she'd been there herself, caring for her mother and her mother-in-law and an older cousin—and, at one point, all three of them at the same time while also raising her two children.

"Mary Ann, I remember screaming at my son when he was eight years old, for no reason," Eileen said. "I was trying to maneuver my mother and my older cousin down a ramp in their wheelchairs, and he was helping me. All the poor kid did was ask me what we were having for dinner that night."

I had to laugh, picturing the scene. It was all too familiar. I no longer had much time, or patience, for anything or anyone that didn't have to do with me or Mom. I'd become selfish in a very strange way. Cindy and Diane joined the conversation, and it took a turn toward that elephant-in-the-room question of "when."

"I don't know," I said honestly. "I know we're getting closer to that, but I always thought it would take some sort of catastrophe, like a broken bone or pneumonia. As in, from the hospital to the nursing home, like my grandma; not from the house to the nursing home."

"That's for the unenlightened," Eileen said levelly.

For a moment no one said anything. Then Diane quoted from T. S. Eliot. "'This is the way the world ends, not with a bang but a whimper,'" she said solemnly.

I felt a strange relief upon hearing this, as I was hoping for some kind of out. Mom had already tried to give me one, and I had rejected it.

A few days before my dinner with my friends, Mom was having an "on" day. We were in her bedroom recovering from our latest bath-time adventures when she asked me to count the skirts in her closet. I asked her why.

"Because I think I have more than enough to go to the home, and that's where I belong," she said firmly.

"No, it's not, Mom, you're fine here," I said with as much conviction as I could muster. I was saying it, but I wasn't feeling it.

"The home" is where Mom stayed for nine days while we took a family vacation during the summer of 2016.

"You'll be swell, you'll be great," we assured Mom just before we brought her to a local nursing home before our trip, sounding like we were starring in some twisted reprisal of the Broadway musical *Gypsy*. And you know what? Mom was swell, she was great. Everyone loved her, and she even made a friend. They were sitting together in companionable silence after dinner when we arrived to bring Mom home. Sitting there and staring at each other blankly and smiling, they were like two impeccably coiffed and dressed halves of the same coin.

During the short ride back to our house, Mom expressed her happiness at returning home. I thought about all the things Mom would be happy about. Reuniting with "her" cat, Junior, an overstuffed allergy-inducer that she loves to bits. Getting up later in the morning and having me bring breakfast to her room. Enjoying the meals I cooked for her and complimenting me even on the ones I considered edible at best. Sleeping in her own bed. Enjoying the ins and outs and goings-on of her grandchildren and their friends. Just being a part of our lives, instead of hearing about things secondhand.

"And we're happy you're coming home," John said. For a second, I thought he was just being nice.

But you know what? John *was* happy. I could see it in his eyes. I was the one with a pit in my stomach. I tried to make it go away by reminding myself that life with Mom certainly had its high points.

After I learned a new move at Zumba or got a new hairdo, I always bounded upstairs for a show and tell with Mom. "Ooh, that's great!" Mom would say. She was still my best friend, my trusted confidante, and my biggest supporter.

At that time, I felt like I still needed her under my roof, sharing my life with me. But now, despite my best efforts, that feeling was diminishing.

I latched onto Diane's statement. Nothing lasts forever, I reminded myself later that night. But I also knew that, for things to change, someone or something had to give.

I hoped that it would be something, and not someone. But I had a feeling it would be someone, and that someone would be me. As in, this is the way the world ends. With a whimper. Or maybe with a wimp.

Chapter Thirty-Three

Side by Side

BESIDES THE OFT-MALIGNED MONTH OF MARCH, WHAT else "comes in like a lion and goes out like a lamb"?

Me, apparently.

And who, may I ask, comes in like a lamb and goes out like a lion?

I think you can venture a guess.

Shortly after my mom moved in during the summer of 2014, a neighborhood acquaintance named Joe was walking past the house as he often does with his adorable beagle, Charlie Brown. I told Joe about my mom living with us, and he nodded his head knowingly.

"My mother-in-law lived with us for twenty years," he said, and my jaw fell. I shouldn't have been that surprised, really. Joe is the kind of guy who would give you the shirt off his back. We shared a few lines of conversation, and then Charlie began tugging, impatient to get to the tree down the block. Joe started to walk again, then held Charlie back for just a moment.

"Promise me something," he said. "Promise me that when it gets to be too much for you, you'll do what my wife and I did and get your mother into a good nursing home. And when you do, you can tell yourself that Joe from down the street says it's okay. Because it will be, really."

"Okay, Joe," I agreed readily, partly to free Charlie from waiting. At the time, I knew that Joe had given me an incredible gift. And I had every confidence that I would never feel compelled to open it.

You know what they say about the best-laid plans. I had nothing against nursing home care. My grandma Anna entered a nursing facility when her need for care exceeded what Mom was able to provide. My mom's siblings had stepped in and done what a devoted family does best—they worked to craft a better situation for their mom and for their sister. The three of them did their research, and Uncle Gabe discovered a beautiful facility in Andover, New Jersey. It was what my father would call "a hike," over an hour from our home. But there was no denying this place was worth the trip.

Each time we visited, we were treated to the sight of nurses and aides in their starched pink and white uniforms. They greeted us warmly and treated Grandma with reverence. I recall my mother crying after we returned to the car following our first visit to Grandma in Andover. It took me a minute or two to realize, to my relief, that they were tears of gratitude.

Having had that experience, I certainly had no problem reassuring people who had either placed their parent in a nursing home or were thinking seriously about taking that step.

"Nursing homes exist for a reason," I said. At the time I believed I was being sincere. But now, with my own situation beginning to unravel, I had to wonder. I didn't want to be the person who put my mom in a nursing home. Assisted living sounded much more palatable, but I knew we couldn't afford it. I felt bad about that, not that it was my fault. I also felt bad about the levels of care and companionship I was providing for Mom, which were my fault. I was doing what needed to be done, with no nice extras.

Mom looked forward to the rare occasions when we hired Carol as her caregiver for the day. Carol came equipped with slices of homemade breads and cakes and dinnertime meals that included plenty of fruits and veggies. On the other hand, I was cranking out the same meals time after time, and grudgingly at that. Carol also made pleasant conversation with my mom, which she would recount for me at the end of each visit. I was pleased, but I had to wonder why these good times were no longer happening for me and Mom. I told myself that perhaps we both just needed a long break from one another. As luck would have it, my daughter's college graduation in the spring of 2016 provided us with that opportunity.

Ever the good sport, Mom went willingly into the local nursing home for respite care the day before we were to leave for Veronica's graduation in Baltimore, Maryland. She'd been to this nursing home a few times before, most recently during Greg's graduation weekend. Each time, we'd had a seamless transition: Mom goes into the home; Mom stays for a few days; we pick her up; we chat in the car on the way back to our house and are relieved to discover that once again she has enjoyed the food and the activities. But when asked, usually by John, Mom says readily that yes, she is very happy to be coming home.

But this time, we were in for a surprise.

On my end, I embarked on the three-day trip to Loyola University in Maryland feeling almost euphoric. I figured this stemmed from the fact that I had brushed aside comments from close friends—concerned for both me and for Mom—that perhaps her care was "getting beyond me." One person had even suggested that I leave Mom in the facility after respite care had ended, for a smoother transition.

"Why bring her home, only to bring her back in again?" she said.

That statement gave me pause, I will admit. I was worried about Mom falling again in my home, as she'd done a few weeks before when I turned my back and she tumbled onto the floor while trying to take off one of her knee-high stockings. She was unhurt, but I was badly shaken.

"Knee highs are *banned* from the kingdom!" I yelled at her, only half joking. Yes, things were heading a bit downhill. But I was determined to see this through.

"Nope, I've got this," I told all of my well-meaning advisers. I managed to convince myself that I believed it. If Mom was Daisy-Head Maisie's egg, I was Horton. I thought about "Side by Side," a song that Mom and I used to sing together when I was a young girl. "In all kinds of weather, what if the sky should fall, just as long as we're together, it doesn't matter at all."

But here is what happened. John and I had unwittingly booked ourselves into a pet-friendly hotel outside of Baltimore for the duration of graduation weekend. I couldn't believe it. I'm allergic to dog hair. On most other occasions, a misstep of this magnitude would cause me to have a meltdown. But this weekend was about my daughter and her achievements. I wasn't going to let this disappointment bring me down.

Sure, my eyes looked puffy in some of the photographs taken the first day of our stay. But that didn't matter so much when I discovered a very pleasant surprise. A convention and exhibition for the owners of borzois—also known as Russian wolfhounds—was being held at our hotel.

I consider borzois to be the most beautiful animals on the planet. They have very lush coats, so I could never own one. But I just adore their sweet faces, regal bearing, and gentle nature. We encountered these beautiful animals around every corner as we walked through the hotel. Borzois here. Borzois there. Borzois *everywhere*.

The weekend of the borzois put me in a whimsical frame of mind. I relaxed more than I had in a long while and felt ready for anything. What I wasn't expecting, however, was a revelation.

The revelation was this—that all of the people surrounding the borzois, from owners to groomers to handlers to helpers, had smiles on their faces pretty much twenty-four seven. Each of them had the glow of passion. They were completely absorbed in their animals and the care they required. I found myself admiring their selfless devotion. And I had to face a sobering reality.

I had lost my passion for caring for Mom. I was no longer devoted to her. My will to persevere had been clouding the issue. But now my vision was clear, and this is what I saw:

Me sighing as I entered Mom's room each morning, dreading the cleaning of the commode—which had once seemed like a blessing but had now become an unwelcome intrusion.

Mom getting upset with me because I refused to bring her downstairs on a day when I had a ton of work to do and a friend coming over for coffee.

Me getting incensed when Mom complained that the water was too hot or too cold during a bath, and me telling Mom that if she would *just stop complaining*, the whole blasted process would go a lot faster.

Mom pitching forward and stumbling as I helped her through the hallway and up or down the stairs, and me feeling like she was going to end up giving me a heart attack—and me telling her so.

Here was the bottom line.

There were increasingly more days when I wished Mom could be elsewhere. Even worse, I suspected she was feeling the same way.

I told John about my revelation the night before we were to head back to New Jersey.

"You're not a professional caregiver, and it *has* gotten past you," he said. "There's no shame in it."

I did feel ashamed. On the ride home, though, I thought seriously about taking the "smooth transition" advice I had been given. I thought about not having to fetch Mom's meals or supervise while she brushed her teeth. I thought about the freedom I would have and how exhilarating it would feel.

But once I returned home and stepped into my house, I got cold feet. There was Mom's spot on the sofa, with the blanket she had crocheted just a few years ago folded carefully over it. There was "her" cat, snoozing on her bed and awaiting her arrival. There were her English muffins on the kitchen counter, just waiting to be toasted and buttered imperfectly by me and greatly appreciated by her. The relief I felt on the ride home turned to shame. I panicked. I was scheduled to pick Mom up the following day!

I started grasping at straws, hoping that I would get some sort of sign to point me in the right direction. I paced. I prayed. I made myself extra-strong coffee and cried into the mug when I realized it said "World's Greatest Grandma" on it. Somehow I pulled myself together and I prayed again. Finally my mind stopped racing long enough for me to receive an answer.

It was not the clear directive I was searching for, but a stop-gap measure. I am at heart a woman of inaction, so the answer was tailor-made. And the answer was this. I didn't want to rip off the bandage, so I needed to buy some time. I immediately arranged for Mom to stay in the nursing facility for a few more days.

John agreed with this plan. "It's the right choice," he said. "It will let us think hard about what we want to do."

Of course, I dreaded what I needed do the next morning, which was head right over to the nursing home and tell Mom she would be there longer than expected. I was frantic as I entered the lobby and walked smack into the director of the facility.

"What if she wants to come home right away?" I asked, restraining myself from grabbing onto the director's shoulder and asking for a hug.

She eyed me sympathetically and with concern. I'm sure I looked disheveled and wild-eyed, and it struck me that maybe the concern in her eyes was for her own well-being. Maybe she was thinking she should have thought of a safer profession—dentist at the local zoo, perhaps.

"Tell her it's for a few days, and she'll understand," she said.

I walked with trepidation into the common room, where Mom sat in her wheelchair dressed in her black skirt and emerald green blouse, her hair combed and her cheeks pink. I flushed with shame when I realized that for the past few months, I had hidden Mom's makeup bag in a back corner of her closet. I had become unwilling to apply her powder and lipstick as she had every day of her life.

"Hi!" Mom said when I stood in front of her. She was so radiant, she stopped me in my tracks. I spotted her aide sitting at a nearby window, beaming her approval.

"She looks beautiful," I said, and the three of us smiled at one another. I was aware that I was trying to buy time. I finally sat down and prepared to justify my selfish decision to my beautiful mother.

Mom beat me to the punch. "Mary Ann, I need to stay here," she said.

I was annoyed. Had the director gone behind my back and told Mom of my decision? Was that why she was so confident that Mom would be fine?

"Who told you *that*?" I said.

"No one told me anything," Mom said. "You can't take care of me anymore. It's too much. It's time. And I'm happy here."

And then Mom related a story.

She had told one of the aides at the nursing facility about my caring for her.

"They take good care of me," she said, as she often did.

But this time Mom didn't get the usual reaction of "Isn't that nice!"

"Oh, my God!" was what the aide said, according to Mom. Mom, whose memory for incidents and details had pretty much flown the coop, had managed to remember this.

After Mom related the story, it was as though time was standing still. I looked into Mom's brown-gray eyes and saw an acceptance that was almost profound in its purity. I may not have had siblings to help me with a decision that needed to be made. But I had a wise ally in this anonymous aide. I felt profoundly blessed and once again said a silent prayer of thanks for the strong women in the world. In this case, Mom and the mystery aide.

We sat there and faced each other like two soldiers who had done their best to win a battle and then had to concede defeat. Or was it defeat? My mom, with her infinite wisdom and strength and innate kindness, made it feel like a victory. I was breathless with admiration.

I suddenly felt energized. I asked Mom a quick succession of questions, lowering my voice while trying to fight back tears.

"How's the food?"

"Good!"

"Do you like the nurses?"

"Yes!"

"Are you doing activities?"

"I think so! I can't remember."

"Are you sleeping well?"

"Oh wait, I like playing bingo! Now I remember!"

"That's good! Are you sleeping well?"

"Yes . . . well, off and on, just like at home."

The word *home* hit me hard. How could Mom not want to come home? Of course she wanted to come home. The one question I wanted to ask Mom that day but didn't dare was, "Won't you miss us?" Because I both knew the answer and dreaded thinking about it. Of course she would miss us. She would miss her pretty room. She would miss looking out of her window at our garden. She would miss the cat. She would miss the kids. She would miss her life as the woman who was so proud and grateful that her daughter and son-in-law wanted her under their roof.

But she knew what needed to happen, and she was being the bigger person by insisting on it. And that was it. Mom was right, as always. She was correct years ago when she told me I was my father's daughter. I fought it, partly because I admired my mom so much. I wanted to be like her. But I don't have her strength, or her fighting spirit. Like my dad, I tend toward introspection and often feel melancholy. I nurture my sadness and wrap it around me like a well-worn sweater. And I had, indeed, been so very sad during the past six months. Mom could see it in my eyes. I had never been able to hide anything from her. So once again, she had been compelled to turn the tide for me by showing me the way.

On that day, in that nondescript room in the nursing home, I felt just like I did when I was a sad young teenager and Mom took my hand to dance the Lindy. "Just do what I'm doing," she said then. "Follow my lead."

I walked out of the nursing home with my head held high. No matter what people said when I told them the big news, I could counter by saying, "Mom wanted it this way."

I didn't have the nerve to open the gift Joe had given me so long ago. As it turned out, I didn't have to. Mom did it for me.

A week after Mom moved into the nursing home, John and I arrived for one of our evening visits. It was Memorial Day weekend, and Mom was in the common room seated with two other ladies, Betty and Mary, who offered us polite hellos. It was obvious to us that Mom was well-loved by everyone in her facility, just as my grandma Anna had been in hers. I was so happy to see my mom. I miss her. I miss her like crazy. I never expected, although I should have, that when Mom moved out she would take the calm in the eye of the storm—the Josephine Zone—with her.

"Now I have to drive fifteen minutes each way to bask in the 'Zone,'" I half joked recently to a friend.

"How was your day, ladies?" John asked. Mom smirked as Betty and Mary giggled. Handsome John was always a hit with the women. Mom and I exchanged a conspiratorial glance. John loves an audience, and we could already tell he was in rare form.

"Did you have your Memorial Day BBQ?" he continued.

"I don't know, did we?" Betty answered, looking at the others questioningly. Mary and my mom shrugged and smiled. This compelled John, who should have been a news anchor, to read the entire BBQ menu off of a nearby flyer.

"Well, it says here that you had BBQ pork and creamed corn and salad and cake," John answered. The ladies were silent, and I held my breath. John and I both enjoy bantering with my mom and her sister, but I worried. Maybe with these women, who were pretty much strangers to us, he might have crossed the line. Then Betty spoke up.

"Well, if you say so!" she said, and we all laughed.

As John and I left that evening, I glanced back at Mom. She appeared relaxed and happy and well cared for, and Betty wheeled her chair closer to Mom. There they sat, side by side.

Chapter Thirty-Four

The Reckoning

I THOUGHT IT WOULD BE THAT EASY.

At first I was exhilarated by the thought of getting my freedom back, thanks to Mom's successful placement in the nursing home. Her mostly easy adjustment, and ours, seemed like a miracle. Then the real world, with all of its demands and expectations and disappointments, came rushing back in to fill the void that Mom's care had left. In the process, I somehow got turned upside down. However, like most unpleasant things, it turned out to be instructive.

While in the midst of Mom's caregiving, I had promised myself something: that I would take to my bed for a week if she "went away," either to a nursing home (which I never thought would happen), or to heaven (which I did). My gut told me I would need that time to rest and meditate on my next step, which I hoped would be gainful employment. I knew my time spent caregiving had impacted our finances, and I wanted to get myself back into the workforce, whether it meant supplementing my part-time job as a press release writer or exploring full-time positions.

The ink on the contract I signed for Mom's nursing home care was barely dry when life got in the way and I got distracted. Socializing, commiserating, and taking care of everyone but myself became my priority. When I realized I had not done what my gut instincts told me to, I felt angry. Then I lost my focus, and my resolve as well. Soon I became depressed, assuming life had short-changed me when, in fact, I had short-changed myself.

Adding to my general state of malaise was the fact that I had equated elder care to childbirth. I assumed that all of the stress and worry I'd faced when caring for Mom would somehow be forgotten once she was delivered safely into the nursing home, just as the joy of holding your newborn baby (hopefully) helps you put aside everything you've gone through in the months and hours and minutes before. Everything I accomplished regarding Mom's care in my home became a blur. If you asked me to tick off a list of chores I performed every day for three years, I would not know where to begin. But here's where I made a miscalculation: I hoped/assumed that *every* problem surrounding me while I cared for Mom would leave the building when she did. Instead, large and small issues that I had brushed aside began to fester. I wasn't sure what the future held, and I was frightened. I began my cycle of walking and crying, crying and walking. Here we go again, I thought. Yet I could not seem to stop my unraveling. I wasn't feeling my usual satisfaction when kayaking, swimming at the beach, or listening to live music. These had formerly been activities I cherished. Now it was as though my clothes were showing up without me.

In my despair, I even wrote my first work of short poetry, which I guess would qualify as an amateurish attempt at a haiku.

Happiness, where have you gone . . .

You never call, you never write.

Yup. I was losing it.

In the weeks and months following Mom's absence from our home, I prayed for guidance on more than a few occasions. I always received the same message: work harder. On what? I wondered. I was indeed slacking off, with the excuse that I had just been through a lot with my mom. My part-time job writing press releases for local schools would not start up again until September, and I needed to find an additional source of income. Yet here it was midsummer, and I hadn't taken any steps in that direction. I was still accepting every invitation to sit on the beach with friends or take walks or meet for coffee. I knew these events were half-hearted attempts at regaining my happiness, and unproductive. Yet I couldn't seem to help myself.

Part of the problem was, I didn't know where to begin. I had been out of the full-time work force for over twenty years. As a helper to my aging parents and then a full-time caregiver, I wondered where all the time had gone. I recalled a conversation I'd had with my mother-in-law Dolly when I was in my mid-twenties and working in New York City. Dolly had cared for one elderly relative after another while raising her sons and was getting ready to begin an administrative assistant position at a nearby insurance company after an almost thirty-year absence from the work force.

"I'm scared to death," she confided.

"You'll be fine," I told her dismissively. "Whatever you do, it's got to be better than folding laundry every day."

When Dolly still looked worried and concerned, I felt frustration rather than pity.

Now I was in the same position and feeling just as frightened as Dolly had. Experience, as they say, is the best teacher. I did not know where to begin.

"You must feel wonderful about the terrific job you did with your mom," was what I heard from those close to my situation.

But I didn't feel wonderful. I felt lost and unproductive. I wondered about opportunities I had missed to broaden my horizons, whose narrowness had once seemed cozy and comforting, especially when Mom first moved in with us. What could be wrong with a small, simple life? I wondered at the time.

Ironically, with Mom now settled in elsewhere, I felt even more constricted. I envied those who had moved on while I had been stuck in neutral. I felt like the walls were closing in on me.

One day about two months after Mom had moved into the nursing home, I decided to take the initiative and work on something. I settled on a plan to sit on the sofa and stream episodes of *Homeland* while playing Candy Crush Saga. Yes, I know that this would not have been God's choice. But in my negative frame of mind, it seemed like the safe one. It was, I reasoned, a starting point. "You're doing so well," my messages from the Candy Crush app read, appearing in happy fluffy clouds as I munched on a granola bar. Ah, this was living, right?

Uh, wrong. After a long while I realized with a jolt that I had been sitting on my sofa watching but not really watching a television show and playing a game on my tablet as though my life depended on it for the entire afternoon. It had been a full three hours or more, by my reckoning. The sudden shame caused me to jump up from the sofa, determined to do something, anything, to make myself productive. Perhaps I would fold the laundry that had been sitting in the basket for a full four days. Eureka! But I hadn't realized that one of my feet had fallen asleep (from sheer boredom, perhaps?). I watched in horror as the offending foot—my right one—folded under my ankle. My body, somehow and unfortunately fully upright thanks to the spring I still had in my aging knees, tilted dangerously to the left. Holding my tablet in the air as though it were a baby, I fell full force onto my left side—with the top of my head missing the glass door leading to the outdoor deck by perhaps an inch.

I had been spared that, at least; but, upon snapping out of my shock, I realized that my right foot was still asleep and my right ankle was throbbing. I had no choice but to lie on the floor, looking up at the snack table littered with granola bar wrappers and empty bottles of iced tea—the lingering evidence of my lack of purpose—while waiting a full fifteen minutes for the feeling in my foot to come back. I filled the time by crying.

I finally limped into the kitchen for a glass of water and realized I had sprained my ankle. I dealt with the incident, and my injury, in the way I had adopted over the years: I denied the extent of my suffering. "I'm fine," I insisted to John when he arrived home from work and noticed that my right ankle was swollen and red and angry as it threatened to burst over the top of my sneakers. I hadn't even bothered to wrap it, as John noted.

"If you say so," John said, knowing instinctively when to back off after almost thirty-five years of marriage.

I pulled myself together enough to host a graduation party for Veronica the next day. I told no one—not even John or Veronica—about the role endless streaming and Candy Crush had played in my injury. But near the end of the graduation celebration, I confided the events of the day before to a close friend.

"Did you consider that when you received a message that God wants you to work hard, He actually meant *on yourself?*" she said. My shocked expression caused her to laugh.

"I've been selfish enough; I haven't even looked for a job," I confessed.

Fortunately, my friend provided absolution. "I promise that if you take care of yourself first, the rest will follow," she said.

Permission to be selfish, with hope for a better tomorrow. What a refreshing concept.

The following Monday I finally made the call I'd been meaning to for weeks. I scheduled an appointment with a local chiropractor/acupuncturist recommended to me by a friend. I'd had neck and back pain for years thanks to scoliosis, and it had recently gotten much worse. I figured that tackling that issue would be a good first step toward self-care. I used my friend's words to bolster my confidence. *Trust me, you deserve it.*

During my first visit, I lay on a padded examination table with my stomach facing the floor, my feet raised on a large rectangular pillow, and my face cradled in a soft terry-covered pillow shaped like a circle. Hot pulses both stimulated and calmed the angry muscles in my upper back, and needles had been positioned carefully in my neck to help ease the shock of the pain, which I felt at least ten times a day when I turned my head sharply for any reason. Something about being in this environment and being cared for in this way compelled me to cry and release all the negative emotion I'd felt over the past few months. But a steel mechanism held the table up just a few feet below my exposed face, and I feared my salty tears would cause it to rust. Before too long, I heard the timer ding, and the doctor—an earth-mother type who immediately made me feel comfortable—returned to prepare me for the next step of chiropractic treatment. To my dismay, my face was wet when she turned me on to my back.

"Oh," I said, embarrassed.

"Your sinuses must be draining, that's good!" she said kindly.

I smiled and thanked God that I had found the person I had been searching for without realizing it. A nonjudgmental healer.

My positive experience bolstered my resolve to get to the heart of what was causing me to be so unhappy. I wasn't sure what it was exactly, but I was fairly certain it wasn't what some of my friends had been guessing:

"Maybe you feel like a failure, but you shouldn't."

"You miss taking care of your mom, and that's understandable. It's as though you've lost a job."

"You worry about her in that place and wonder if you made the right choice."

No, no, and no. Well, maybe. Four days after my initial treatment, I paid another scheduled visit to the chiropractor/acupuncturist. I lay on my back with needles carefully positioned in my face to help my sinuses drain. My practitioner set a timer and left the room with a swish of her batik-patterned skirt and closed the door. The lights had been dimmed and soothing piano music was being piped in, and by all rights I should have been very relaxed. But for some reason my heart began racing and a feeling of dread came over me. I felt like I was sinking, and flashes began hitting my tightly shut eyes as though someone had turned on a strobe light. In my sudden state of fright, I thought about calling out for the doctor, whose sandals I could hear thwacking as she walked down the hall and passed my door:

Um, Dr. C.? Dr. C? Could you come in here for a moment?

But, of course, I didn't. It wasn't just that I didn't want to make a scene. I was afraid that if I opened my mouth, one of the carefully positioned needles would fall out, possibly ruining my doctor's hard work and the effectiveness of my treatment.

I took deep breaths to calm myself down, and the flashing lights turned into a scene from my childhood. I had returned home from a birthday party for a second-grade classmate. It was the first real event I had attended since entering grammar school. Standing in our small living room with its rustic charms—wood paneling, large windows, oiled linoleum flooring, and a surprisingly high ceiling—I was bursting to tell Mom of all the games we had played at the birthday party. I was thinking about where to start when Mom upended me with a statement.

"I bet you were the prettiest girl there!" she exclaimed confidently. She stood there, with her minimal makeup expertly applied and her hair perfectly coiffed and her dress freshly ironed, while I tried my best to give this some serious consideration.

Before that point I had given some thought to my appearance, wishing I had my father's blue eyes and my mother's even and expressive facial features, rather than my mother's brown-gray eyes and my father's handsome yet imperfect face, with its large nose and sharp cheekbones. But I had never before thought about where I ranked on the prettiness scale with regard to my classmates, with whom I had just spent a wonderful afternoon. With my mother looking on expectantly, I tried to rack my brain. Somewhere above the friendly Sue but below the already willowy and exotic Liz? Yes, that could be right. In other words, average. Right smack in the middle, in the comfort zone. But, eager to please my mom, I answered, "Yes!" And Mom's face lit up with a smile.

On that day, in that small living room, something inside of me changed forever. I had taken up Mom's mantle, and almost every step I took from then on was toward being better than someone else. In my mind, I thought I could perhaps become the prettiest or smartest or nicest girl in the room if only I worked harder at it. I began to believe this was the reason to wake up every morning; if you couldn't improve in some way every day, what was the point? The quest for perfection, or at least some sort of superiority, it seemed to me, was the key to happiness. I began treating it as such. And I assumed that my parents—with their shared high standards for appearance and behavior—felt the same way.

I had been raised in an impeccably clean home, with parents who kept to themselves as though they needed nothing more than one another and, of course, me. Sure, setting the bar high caused them to be judgmental and closed off to others—society's braggers, liars, thieves, complainers, risk-takers, and all-out "dopes" to name a few. Yet the fact that they were surrounded by my dad's ever fun-loving family helped to make up for lack of outside friendships. My factory-worker parents managed to buy a home and put food on the table, and having little money for life's extras—vacations or dinners out—never really managed to spoil our fun. We were insular, self-sufficient, and peaceful.

Peaceful. The word stuck in my mind. Suddenly I did feel peaceful. I realized my heart had stopped racing. The scene from my childhood had actually morphed into a soothing glow. I felt as though my body was being raised up. I half wondered if my doctor had quietly reentered and was lifting the table. But I was alone with my thoughts. Blessedly alone with my thoughts.

There were no tears on my face that day when my doctor returned to the room. Just a smile and a feeling of determination that I hadn't experienced for a while. A thread of knowledge had been dangled in front of me, and I was determined to follow it. Yes, I did need to work harder. *On myself.*

I headed to a nearby coffee shop and sat at a table near the window. I needed some time to think. I continued riding on my current train of thought and ended up realizing that, despite their high standards, my parents did not always have an easy time of it. I had always described them as happy, but in reality they'd had their struggles, especially after Dad lost almost all of his vision and they had to move to Long Branch. Long accustomed to being in a home and enjoying the sights and sounds of a large backyard and being surrounded by family and by friendly neighbors, they lived out their days in a one-bedroom apartment with somewhat infrequent visits by me. I was too busy, I told myself at the time.

I could have done better. A lot better. But the pressure I felt when my parents moved to Long Branch and relied on me for transportation and entertainment was enormous. My insecurities sometimes prevented me from making my best efforts on their behalf. I felt that if I couldn't be a perfect companion to my aging parents, why try? Equating my mother's happiness with her quest for perfection, I once again decided I could never live up to her standards. And so I put my parents on the back burner. I treated them well, of course, but I know I could have done more.

During my visits to Long Branch, which I sometimes enjoyed and sometimes dreaded, my mother often reminded me about how much Dad missed his house, his yard, and his sister Betty. But I now realized it was my mom who really must have been struggling during those twelve years in Long Branch, trapped with her thoughts and nearing the end of her life in that sometimes dreary and empty-feeling apartment. My mother had long harbored dreams of traveling to an exotic island, perhaps on a cruise ship. So many of her wishes—to travel, to have more children, to live in a larger house she could easily entertain in—had gone unfulfilled. How, I now wondered, had she managed to wake up every day and take her shower and brew her coffee and face lonely hours spent staring out of the window at the ocean while my father dozed peacefully until noon? Even when awake, my dad was a man of few words. And, as he grew older, his anxiety increased and he became more demanding. I thought about how just even a few more visits from me would have lifted her spirits and eased her loneliness. She could not possibly have been happy during the Long Branch years. Not even somewhat happy, which was what I had assumed at the time. But now, sipping on a cappuccino and watching the passersby, I felt remarkably clear-headed. Perhaps Mom hadn't been happy at all. And yet, hadn't she given the impression that she was?

It was then it dawned on me. High standards and the quest for the best were a large part of my mother's persona. But they were not, as I had assumed, the key to her happiness. In fact, I had confused happiness with contentment. Mom was not always happy, not even somewhat. But she was content. My misery was based on the assumption that I could not find contentment without happiness. And I couldn't be happy unless everything was perfect. But when I finally decided to think hard about it, my mother had proved this wrong, and on every single day of her life. That's why people were drawn to her and admired her so. Mom's high standards were a part of her persona, but they played a distant second fiddle to her unshakable faith; *that* was what defined her. Life had indeed let my mother down at times. But, in her mind, God never had. Mom didn't wake up every day and accomplish her dreary routine because she hoped for perfection or improvement. She woke up every day and took on the world because she fully believed in God's plan for her. And if other people disappointed her, well, that was part of God's plan as well. My mother always wanted the best in life, for herself and for everyone else. Sure, she sometimes complained when things didn't turn out her way. But she accepted it as God's will. She never lost her faith, in me or anyone else. My mother was the queen of high standards, but also the queen of second chances. She believed in everyone's potential. As her friend Carmen had tried to tell me so many years ago, when I had been too arrogant to listen, Mom never gave up on anyone. I shook my head in disbelief when I realized how stupid I'd been, and for so long.

My dad's voice suddenly appeared in my head. "You got your signals crossed," I heard him say. I had screwed up. I had put happiness before contentment and high standards before faith. But my mother hadn't. If I could only look past her sometimes critical judgments of me or my actions, I would see someone who really did believe in my potential. Someone who would always love and support me, no matter what I said or did or didn't say and do. Someone who believed that God's plan for her included one struggling daughter who nevertheless was trying to do her best for everyone with the tools she had been given. Immediately I knew where I needed to go, and I knew what I needed to do.

"Oh, why are you here?" Mom said when I entered the day room on the fourth floor of the nursing home.

"I missed you," I said, kissing the top of her head. I greeted her friend group, which had grown by one with the addition of a funny man called Mr. K. He reminds me of my dad, and I know that my mom feels the same way. "Take good care of my friend,"

Mr. K. once told me when I arrived to fetch mom for attendance at her sister's birthday party. I think they might like one another. And if so, that's good.

It was a sunny day, and I walked to the window to catch a glimpse of the Swimming River. Popular with kayakers and nature lovers, the Swimming River is an estuary that flows near the front of the nursing home's large property. Mom's friend Mary almost always asks me for a report on what the river is doing. At low tide, the water becomes murky and muddy and appears to move lazily in a million different directions. At high tide, however, the water flows somewhat clearer and green, with a purpose that makes it sparkle.

"How's the river?" Mary asked.

"It's at high tide, I think," I answered.

"I wish that we could see it from here," Mom said as her friends all nodded in agreement.

"Yes, I wish the windows were larger," I said, knowing full well that full-length windows in a nursing home day room were an accident waiting to happen. But we could dream, couldn't we? Then I had an idea.

"Mom, do you want to go outside?" I asked.

"Oh, it's too much trouble," she demurred.

"No, it's not," I said. I often felt guilty about taking Mom outside, since her lady friends had few visitors and were therefore sort of stuck in the day room with people like me to fill them in on the weather, the river, and local and world events. Most times I just stayed in the day room with Mom and her friends, watching television and doing my best to keep up a conversation that included all of them. But my days of perfection, of trying to take care of everyone and everything, were nearing an end. I wasn't in charge. God was. What a relief, I thought. Losing a power I actually never had was an unburdening of the highest order. I couldn't change the situation for any members of Mom's adorable posse. But I needed to provide my own mother with a change of pace. Baby steps, I reminded myself. Baby steps.

As I guided Mom's wheelchair through the lobby, I thought about a meeting I'd had recently with some of the staff members.

"We're really happy that your mom is here on a permanent basis," the social worker had said. "She's lovely and warm and friendly, and she really adds something for us. It's as though we needed her."

I had been proud and relieved and heartened by that statement. And yet I had been saddened, as well. I needed my mom, too. But she had moved on, in a way. I remembered a day shortly after Mom entered the nursing home, when John and I were arguing over something I can't recall. We were worn out and saddened by saying yet another goodbye to my mom. First it was the dementia that took her away. Then the nursing home.

"Ironically, my mother is faring better than any of us right now," I said angrily during the heat of the disagreement.

Immediately, I felt horrible for expressing envy toward my infirm mother. Mom wasn't necessarily happier in the nursing home than she had been when living with us. Not by a long shot. She just accepted this latest disruption to her life, thanks to her unshakable faith in God. Mom was content because she believed in His plan. Why had I stopped? Or, even worse, had I ever started?

The whoosh of the automatic doors leading to the patio jolted me back to reality. I positioned Mom to face the river and sat on a nearby cushioned wicker sofa. I needed to tell her something, and I wasted no time.

"Mom, I'm really sorry I wasn't there more for you and Dad when you lived in Long Branch."

My mom, who almost always cannot recall what she's eaten for breakfast, reached back into her memory bank and seemed to have no trouble conjuring up the period of time that lasted from 2002 to 2013.

"Well," she said finally. "You did your best." She shrugged and gave me a sideways glance.

And that, as they say, was that. My years of experience with Mom-speak told me she was telling me, without saying so, that she would have done better given the same situation. Most likely she was correct in that assumption. And yes, it made me feel bad. Very bad. But the real message, the one that I could now blessedly decipher, was that she accepted my failings. I swore that just a few seconds ago I had seen contentment on her face along with the sideways glance that always accompanied one of her backhanded compliments. If I wanted to move forward in my life, I had to let go of my fear of not living up to Mom's high standards. That fear had kept me from her when she needed me most. And so, yes, I had screwed up. But I was still breathing. I hadn't been struck by lightning. Best of all, I knew that my mom still loved me in the strong and safe way she always had. I raised my face as the sun shone brightly, warming my imperfect self and giving me a sense of calm and contentment I hadn't felt for a while.

I turned to Mom and saw how peaceful she looked. She had been raised by a highly critical mother but one who also believed in God's plan. The act of reaching for high standards wanted to rule Mom's roost, and my grandmother's as well, but faith always won out. Disappointment, then acceptance. Criticism, then unfailing love and support. I sat there and silently thanked God, as I had many times before, for the sassy and sometimes tough-minded woman sitting next to me. She was His way of providing the best possible mother for me. Mom had bestowed on me the greatest gift you can give anyone. The gift of faith.

Being the prettiest girl at the party or the smartest or the funniest won't guarantee happiness. Or, more importantly, contentment. But you should do your best to *just show up*. If I hadn't achieved perfection or come even close when my parents relied on me for help during the Long Branch years, I had at least showed up at the party. Their party. I smiled at this revelation, and Mom gave me another sideways glance. It appeared she was going to say something and then changed her mind. I was relieved. I was in no mood for conversation, or for the repetitive questions she usually peppered me with.

For the first time in a long time, sitting in silence with me seemed to be enough for Mom. I took her hand, and she surprised me by squeezing mine.

In front of us the sparkling green water of the Swimming River flowed, passing over today's memories and delivering the promise of a fresh new tomorrow.

Acknowledgments

FIRST AND FOREMOST, I WOULD LIKE TO THANK MY HUS-band John and our children Greg and Veronica for their love and patience –especially during the caregiving and writing process. They always picked me up when I fell down, and I am forever grateful for the solicitous care they provided to "Queen Josephine."

I am hugely grateful to the fabulous crew at WiDo Publishing for having faith in my book and guiding me through this process. My editor Tamara Heiner has been spot-on and very patient, and provided humor and hope to me as well. Tamara, you are awesome. Many thanks also to Joseph Jones, my Submissions Editor, and to Editor-in-Chief Karen Gowen. You are all "top-drawer."

I was also blessed with the most energetic and gracious early reader on the planet. Pat Zimel volunteered countless hours to examine my entire first manuscript with a fine-tooth comb. During the many times I met with Pat and discussed her comments, I began to believe in my book. Pat, you are a treasure.

Many thanks to Sara Maris, who created a warm and inviting design for my website, and also to early manuscript readers Robin Kampfe, Andrea Van Dyk, Lisa Luckett, Di Saccoccia, Cindy Egan, Lois Rafferty, Hope Hensler Richardson, Carol

Bruno, and Barbara Zeller. I owe a debt of gratitude to Kathleen Connolly and Tony LoBue, who helped me navigate the business end of writing. I also wish to thank Jamie Turner, Jane Lux, Colleen Smith, Mary Chiarella, Carol Corbett, Angela Jobe, Michelle Mina Scheiber, my Book Group ladies, my Mandrick and D'Annunzio cousins, and many others who believed in the book's potential before I had written a word of it.

It would be impossible to thank everyone individually, but I am endlessly grateful to all of my friends and family members. You've never doubted me, or questioned any of the decisions I made during the caregiving journey. Your kindness has meant the world to me. Now more than ever, I know how very blessed I am.

And finally I give thanks for my mom Josephine. I don't know where I would be without your strength and faith, Mom. There have been many times when I wished I could lend you to friends and acquaintances who were struggling. Just for a while. As you and I both know, too much of either of us is never a good thing. We finally agree on that, and it's enough. I love you to bits.

About the Author

A PROUD NATIVE OF NEW JERSEY, MARY ANN KAMPFE WAS born in Union City and raised in Ridgefield Park. She then lived in Fairview and Union, and settled in Fair Haven. Mary Ann embarked on a career in advertising after graduating from Rowan University, and worked as a copywriter in New York City. She is now a substitute teacher at Red Bank Regional High School.

Mary Ann and her husband John are the parents of two grown children, Greg and Veronica. They enjoy all aspects of the Jersey Shore, and travel throughout the state to spend time with family and friends. They also visit Bar Harbor, Maine as often as they can to enjoy the beauty of the area, especially Acadia National Park. Mary Ann enjoys hiking, swimming, crafting, Zumba, and reading in her spare time.

Dementia Dolls: A Daughter's Story is Mary Ann's first published book. She hopes that it brings laughter and comfort to those caring for a loved one, and honor to those bravely suffering from dementia and Alzheimer's. Readers are encouraged to reach out to Mary Ann through social media and to visit her website, www.elderskelter.net. Speaking engagements and book talks can be arranged by contacting makampfe@aol.com.

CPSIA information can be obtained
at www.ICGtesting.com
Printed in the USA
BVHW031742280619
552245BV00001B/9/P